Full Beds Forever

How To Market Your Care Home In 3 Simple Steps

Simon Beck

DOWNLOAD THE AUDIOBOOK FOR FREE!

READ THIS FIRST

Just to say thank you for choosing my book,
I'd like to give you the audio version for FREE!
Plus a heap of cool bonuses!

TO CLAIM YOUR BONUSES

go to: http://www.carehomemarketingbook.com/bonuses

ISBN: 978-0-9934767-8-5

Table of Contents

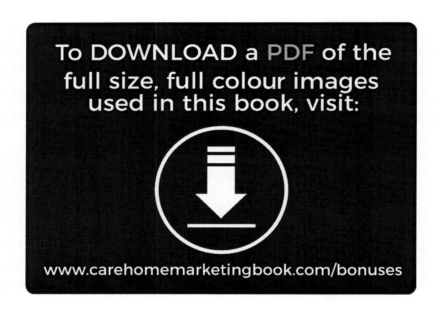

http://www.carehomemarketingbook.com/bonuses

Introduction

The £78,000 Suitcase

Every time someone interested in a place in your care home comes to look around, they're carrying with them a large suitcase stuffed to bursting with £78,000 in used banknotes. Cold, hard cash.

The £78,000 Suitcase

What you do, what you say, and what they see, determines whether they'll hand over all that lovely cash to you, or go down the road and hand it over to your competitors.

Which one would you prefer?

In this book I'm going to show you how to find people who are looking for a place in a care home, and how to make sure their money ends up in your bank account.

Read This First

You might imagine that this book would be in three parts, given its title and the promise of 'three simple steps', but you'd be wrong.

The book is in four parts. Here's why.

To get the best out of a subject you often need a certain level of understanding. For example, I like looking at great works of art, and paintings in particular. The trouble is, I don't really know anything about art, so I just admire the skill of the artists and the scene that the picture depicts.

I'm also a fan of TV art programmes, where an expert explains everything to me.

With an art expert on the case, I know I'm going to find out all about the life of the painter, the politics, and events of the time they lived in, as well as what the painting means. Hopefully, I'll also be entertained and have fun watching along the way.

By watching the TV programme, I move from the superficial to a deep insight of the work, which improves my understanding and enjoyment of it immensely.

Part one of this book gives you the same kind of insight and understanding about some of the crucial marketing concepts that you'll need to get your head around, to get the most out of parts two to four, which deal with the promised 'three simple steps'.

You may be tempted to skip part one (even I nearly fell asleep writing the very words 'marketing concepts'). However, I urge you not to.

If you're truly serious about making your care home successful for the long term, or selling it for a handsome profit, it's essential that you understand these concepts.

And, like the art experts, I promise I'll try to make it interesting and entertaining along the way!

So, let's get started.

PART ONE

Important Concepts

Chapter 1

The Money's In The Numbers

Just imagine how great it would be if you knew that all your beds were going to be filled in your care home every single day of the week, every month of the year, and for every year you owned the home.

Just think how good it would be to know that, whatever the financial climate, whatever your Local Authority's funding levels, whatever your competition is doing, and whether you're there or not, you have a list of clients just itching for a place to become available in YOUR home.

Picture having peace of mind and freedom from financial pressures and worry; money to invest in your business to improve your service, or to fund expansion; time off to spend with your family, take a holiday, or just to relax and indulge in your favourite hobby; or perhaps maximising the business' value so that you can sell up, retire, or pursue your lifelong dream.

This is what life will be like for you if you market your care home properly. Effective marketing is the goose that lays the golden egg. It's the keys to the kingdom. It's the difference between success and failure, and it starts with numbers.

Now, before you run screaming from the room at the thought of doing some maths (well, that's my reaction anyway!), this is really good stuff.

And it's easy, so bear with me.

Back To The £78,000 Suitcase

So, what the heck was I on about with that £78,000 suitcase thing?

Well, if your residents stay for an average of three years in your home, and you charge £500 per week, each resident is worth, on average, £78,000 to your business.

This is known as the **average lifetime customer value (LCV),** and it's one of the most important metrics in your business.

You need to know exactly what the actual LCV is for your care home, so let's look at the formula again - and this time, fill in the blanks for your care home.

Average Lifetime Customer Value Formula

First, take the average length of stay in weeks

Then, multiply that by your weekly fee

In our example we have 3 years (156 weeks) x £500 = £78,000

Now, write down your figures

Number of weeks _____

x weekly fee £_____

= £_____

This is your average lifetime customer value

Four Important Notes:

1. When calculating the average length of stay *only include past residents who have now left in your calculations*. Do not include current residents, as their stay is not complete and they'll affect your figures by lowering the average length of stay.

2. If you don't know the average length of stay in your home, make an educated guess for now. This is one of the things you

should be tracking, though.

3. Don't include short term respite or day care in your calculations.

4. If you provide mixed types of care in the same location, calculate the LCV separately for each type of care. For example, separate nursing care from general residential and calculate the LCV for each. It's likely to be quite different because the weekly fee and average length of stay will be different for each.

Why Lifetime Customer Value Is So Important

Before I answer that, let me ask you a question. How much money do you currently spend on marketing your care home?

I ask the audience this question when I'm presenting on stage, and around 60% to 70% of the care home owners present don't spend anything at all.

The rest tend to spend a very modest amount, and a small percentage spend quite a lot.

The latter are usually running the most successful care homes.

Here's another question: if you had an empty bed, and I came to you with a person who wanted a place in a care home, how much would you pay me for that lead?

£5? £50? £100? £500? £1000? £2000?

Not sure?

This is why you need to know how much each customer is worth to you.

Once you understand that each customer is worth £78,000 to your business *you can decide exactly how much of that money you're prepared to spend on attracting a new customer.*

Make sure you're sat down when you read this next bit!

I recommend you be prepared to spend at least 1% to 2% of the lifetime customer value to attract each new resident.

That's £780 to £1560 in our example - *for each and every new resident.*

Now I can understand, if you're used to spending nothing on marketing, that this may come as something of a shock.

In fact, when I reveal this from the stage, I see half the audience turn a deathly pale and visibly wilt into their seats.

But this is the biggest mistake I see care home owners make.

If you can't reliably and predictably spend £x to attract a new customer, you don't have a business.

That may sound controversial, but if your only method of filling your beds is to expect that people will somehow find and choose your care home, your business strategy is 'hope'.

And relying on hope is the worst business decision since Decca Records decided to turn down the Beatles.

How Much Should You Budget For Marketing?

Now you know your lifetime value and you've decided how much of that you can afford to spend on attracting a new client, it's time to put together your marketing budget for the year.

But how much should your marketing budget be?

Well, to calculate that, you really need to know how many new residents you need to attract each year, which is quite easy to work out.

Let's assume you have a 60-bed care home.

Let's also assume that the average length of a resident's stay is three years. Therefore, if your home starts off full, and you don't replace any residents, in three years it'll be empty. On average, you'll lose 20 residents per year.

The formula for calculating how many residents you need to attract each year is the total number of beds divided by the average length of stay.

In our example: 60 beds ÷ 3 years = 20 residents

You now know you need 20 residents. If you've decided you can afford to spend up to £1000 to attract each resident your marketing *budget* becomes £20,000.

Three Important notes:

1. Just because your budget is £20,000, it doesn't necessarily mean you're going to spend all of it.

2. Your marketing budget is not just your advertising budget. It also includes redecorating vacated rooms, staff sales training, and many other items we'll cover later in this book.

3. If you already have vacant beds you need to ADD those to your total marketing budget figure for your *first year.*

    For example, if you already have 10 beds vacant in your 60-bed home, you're going to have to fill those AND the 20 more that will become vacant in the next 12 months, if you're going to get full and stay full.

    So, your first year marketing budget would then be £30,000.

Again, I do realise that if you've never spent a penny on marketing, this could be daunting - so think of it like this: if the 60-bed home in our example charges £500 per week, and it's full, that business is turning over £1.5 million a year.

An annual marketing budget of just £20,000, or even £30,000, to support a £1.5 million-a-year-turnover business, is actually miniscule.

In case you're still not convinced, sign up for our mystery bonus chapter at the link below where I reveal how you can get all your marketing for FREE.

http://www.carehomemarketingbook.com/bonuses

Sound good? O.K. Let's move on.

Chapter 2

A Cautionary Tale

Before we get onto the main course of this book, I would like to issue this stern warning:

In the desert, they wisely say, 'Dig the well before you're thirsty.'

Here's how this applies to your care home.

Time and again, I hear from care home owners in trouble. They're not getting any new residents in. The phone's stopped ringing and they've no idea why, or even noticed, until it's too late.

Here's what's really happened to them, and what *could easily happen to you, if you don't use the techniques in this book to prevent it.*

Let's say there are four care homes in your local area (we'll call them A,B,C,D). Initially, everyone has enough enquiries to keep them full (see Fig. 1).

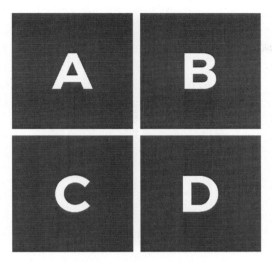

Fig.1 Four happy care homes in a local market

Please visit http://www.carehomemarketingbook.com/bonuses to download a full colour PDF of the images used in this book

Then comes the seismic shift.

All of a sudden, the local authority moves a big chunk of their funding to home care, and the number of funded places instantly shrinks by 20% (see Fig. 2).

Fig.2. The market shrinks by 20%

You'd imagine that everyone suffers a 20% drop in enquiries, as in Fig. 2, yes? Nope. Here's what really happens.

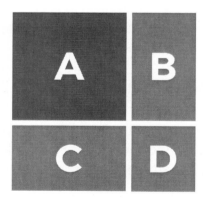

Fig.3 What really happens

Home A is a great home - innovative, with a great reputation, and top-class marketing. They're still everyone's first choice, so they're unaffected.

Homes B and C are good homes, too. But they don't have their marketing sorted, so they're nowhere near as well known as home A. They start to suffer vacancies, and fall below 100% occupancy, which eats away at their profits. Life becomes tough.

Home D is in real trouble. They only get enquiries when A,B and C are full. And they're the castoffs; the scraps; the worst customers that the others don't want.

Occupancy falls catastrophically; money bleeds out of the home's reserves, and they face financial ruin.

That's when I get the distress call.

If you haven't already started to actively market your care home, I urge you to do so NOW. Dig the well before you're thirsty.

It's no use waiting until you've had empty beds for months, you've got no cash left, and the bank manager is breathing down your neck, as he wonders when you're going to pay back all that money he was so eager to loan you.

You won't have the money to invest in it by then, and you'll risk losing everything you've worked for.

Chapter 3

Outside Perception Vs. Inside Reality

One of my first clients was a lovely chap called Peter DeGroot, who had a care home in Exmouth called Rose Lodge.

Peter outsourced the management of the home, and the company concerned had done a terrible job. The staff were demoralised, only 12 of the 24 beds were filled, the infrastructure needed investment, and Peter was left staring into the abyss of potential business failure.

At the time, the home tried to be jack-of-all-trades; it took general residential and dementia category residents. As a result, however, they weren't really looking after the needs of either category as well as Peter wanted.

Compounding his problems was the fact that Exmouth is a small place with a limited amount of prospective clients to draw on. Certainly not enough to fill the home, given its lack of desirability in relation to its local competition.

We sat in the dining room on a warm, sunny day and discussed the options.

I outlined a plan to reinvent the home as a top-drawer specialist dementia care centre; a regional version of a specialist Swiss clinic, or Harley Street practice in London - both of which attract potential clients from all over the world.

This expert specialist care would give people a compelling reason to travel to the home from all over the Devon region, thus solving the lack of potential clients problem.

Peter was already interested in dementia and liked the idea, so we set to work putting the plan into action. And therein lay the first problem.

Within your marketing material, you can portray your business in any way you want. You can make it sound absolutely fantastic, and have people salivating with anticipation at the prospect of doing business with you.

The trouble is, this creates high expectations. Once clients step over the threshold of your care home you'd better make sure that the 'inside reality' lives up to the 'outside perception'. If not, they'll be terribly disappointed, and you'll lose their business.

With Rose Lodge I had the easier job: creating marketing materials that portrayed the home as a specialist dementia care home.

Peter had the much harder task of transforming the home so that the perception and reality matched.

I'm delighted to say that he achieved a remarkable turnaround, and within six months the home was full, and he also had a waiting list of full fee-paying clients eager for a place.

Since then, he's achieved an outstanding CQC report, won several awards, extended the home, and been featured on BBC Radio 4 (but that's another story).

In this book, I'm going to show you how to create great marketing that will have folks craving a place in your home.

However, it's totally pointless and a complete waste of money if your home isn't *actually* a superb home, nor a place where people want to spend the latter part of their life.

You can't make a silk purse out of a sow's ear, as the saying goes. No amount of wonderful marketing will make up for being presented with a sow's ear when you wanted a silk purse - so please make sure your home is a silk purse.

Business Perception Vs Reality

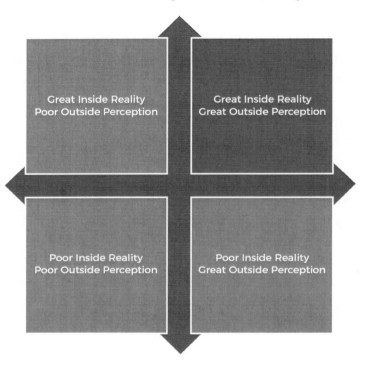

Fig.4 Outside Perception Vs. Inside Reality

Please visit http://www.carehomemarketingbook.com/bonuses to download a full colour PDF of the images used in this book

Take a look at the diagram above. What you're aiming for is the green quadrant, where you have a great inside reality matched by an equally great outside perception.

In fact, in the care industry, most homes I come across are in the 'Great inside reality with poor outside perception' quadrant.

They're really great places that are run by caring and dedicated staff. Trouble is, they do hardly any marketing, and if they do create something, it looks just like everyone else's, including the rubbish homes. The consumer, therefore, has no idea which home to choose.

After reading this book you'll be able to change all that, so your home stands out as a beacon of excellence, the type of place where they'd be crazy if they didn't want to be a resident.

Let's take a look at one of the best ways to achieve that.

Chapter 4

The Importance Of Proof

Picture the scene: you're in the unfamiliar and intimidating surroundings of a law court. Worse still, you're the one sitting in the dock, accused of murder. *You* know you're completely innocent and it's all been a terrible mistake, but the jury don't.

You're terrified. There's a real possibility you'll be sent to prison for the rest of your life, if you're found guilty. Your stomach is turning cartwheels. There's sweat on your brow, and your blood is running like ice through your veins.

Your whole future hangs on the evidence your barrister will present to the court to PROVE your innocence.

If you found yourself in this situation you'd want your barrister to present every possible scrap of evidence that will prove your case.

You'd want them to move heaven and earth to find copious indisputable facts - no matter how small - that ultimately build a weight of evidence so heavy, that the jury simply must conclude you walk free.

The simple truth is, you're facing this situation every day with your potential customers. You want them to consider your care home, and conclude that they'd have to be absolute fools to trust the care of their precious loved one to anyone else.

To do this, you must present a wealth of evidence that proves what a brilliant job you're going to do for them. They must be left in no doubt, and you must find every single thing, no matter how small, that supports your case.

Let's have a look at the types of evidence and proof that you can provide.

Types Of Proof

Here's a list of things you can use as evidence of your brilliance. It's not an exhaustive list, but there's plenty to get your teeth into...

Testimonials
References
Thank-you letters from grateful customers
Case studies
Professional and Government Standards
Professional associations you belong to
Articles and mentions in the media

Awards
Satisfaction surveys
Comparisons with your competitors
Endorsements
Photos and videos
Expertise tests
Training and certification standards
Performance audits
Compliance checklists
Facts and figures
Examples of results, i.e. savings/increases
Books
Charts and graphs
Client lists
Earnings reports
Product demos
Standards lists
Statistics
Test/Lab results

Before we look at some of the most commonly-used in detail, let me address the elephant in the room, with regards to many of these forms of proof - which is *obtaining permission to publish*. You must obtain the correct permissions to use images of, or information about, your residents.

We've found the easiest way to do this is to engineer it into the process of them becoming a resident, by making it a condition of the contract a new resident signs when they take a place in your home.

A clause, to the effect of: 'you agree to photos and videos of you being used from time to time, for promotional purposes'.

Now, I have no legal training, and I am in no way qualified to give you legal advice. I therefore recommend you seek legal advice at all times where appropriate, and especially when drafting the contents of your contract (that's the legal bit covered, so you can't sue me!).

Having said that, at the time of writing, I don't know of anyone who has ever objected to this, especially once you show them the sympathetic and sensitive way you use these materials - which we'll cover in more detail later.

For existing residents, you simply need to explain what you're doing and ask for their permission.

Testimonials And Reviews

Ebay is a massively successful company that has grown from nowhere to the giant it is today, very quickly. There are a number of reasons for this, but chief among them is their ratings system.

On Ebay, your buyers rate you as a seller, and vice-versa. A high rating is a strong indicator that you're trustworthy, that you'll do what you say you're going to do, and that the goods or service you provide will be up to the job.

Isn't that what we all want, especially when we're placing our loved one in the care of others? We want to know, based on true independent evidence, that you'll be as good as your marketing materials say you'll be.

It's the same with Amazon, another massive success. Reviews are everywhere.

Just like Amazon and Ebay, you need to have reviews and testimonials for your home. The more positive reviews you have, the more people will trust you with the care of their loved one.

If it came to the choice between a home that *seemed* good, but which had no reviews, and one that seemed *equally* good, and which was backed up by dozens of glowing reviews and testimonials from happy and grateful relatives, which one would you choose?

www.carehome.co.uk is the primary platform for providing reviews of care homes in the UK. They make it very easy for families and residents to leave reviews about your home, and they now have good measures in place to ensure that the reviews are genuine and that no one is gaming the system.

Another enormous benefit that comes from getting lots of positive reviews on www.carehome.co.uk is that it can directly generate new enquiries for you.

Their website gets a huge amount of web traffic, and it usually occupies the first two to four organic results when you search for a care home on Google.

When someone clicks through to the website from a search, they're presented with the enhanced listings first (these are paid listings), and these are ranked by default, with the highest rated care home at the top of the list.

These days, people make instant judgements about what they find on the net, so you need to be in the top three or four results to get an enquiry.

The 80/20 rule comes into play here (as it does everywhere). The top 20% of homes listed will get 80% of the enquiries. If there are a lot of homes listed in your area, the percentage split might even be 95/5.

There are other websites where people can leave reviews about your home. Two more important ones are: your Facebook page, and your Google My Business page.

The key to success when collection reviews is to make it easy for people to leave them, which each of the above do, and to actually *ask* residents and their families to provide one.

However, if you don't create a system for this, it will fall by the wayside and get lost in the hubbub of daily activity in the home. More on systems later, as all successful businesses run on them.

Thank You Letters From Grateful Customers

Caring for the elderly is an emotive issue. If you're doing it right, the families you deal with will be profoundly grateful and many of them will write to you to tell you so.

Keep these letters in a big file and give it to people to look through when they come to look around the home.

Scan them and publish them on your website and social media profiles. Photocopy them, and include them with the information pack you give to people to take away with them at the end of the show-around. Give them out with brochure requests.

Case Studies

When people purchase a product or service they want it to produce a result they want, but don't have; or to take away a problem they have, but don't want.

Case studies are a brilliant way of demonstrating how you do both. With a case study, you're aiming to show a transformation in the life of the resident.

Before they came to you they were lonely, they couldn't look after themselves, they were unhappy and a burden to their family. They're the problems they and their family have, but don't want.

Now, they have new friends, they get involved in interesting and fun activities; they're looked after 24/7; they're happier, more fulfilled, and have a new-found lust for life, their families enjoy the time they spend with them, instead of it being a chore. They're the results they want, but don't have.

When I talk with staff in our clients' homes, I find many such transformational stories, and you will, too. It doesn't matter if it's nursing care, general residential, dementia, or almost any other type of care you provide.

These stories are often used anecdotally by staff when showing someone around the home, which is a superb use of them.

However, they could also be written down as proper case studies. Or they could be made into video/audio interviews with the resident and/or their family explaining what life was like before moving to the home, and how great it is now they've taken the plunge.

In good care homes, we frequently hear new residents and their families say "I wish we'd done it much sooner.'

When people eventually move into a good care home, they usually find that all their misgivings were completely misplaced - it does literally transform their lives for the better.

Case studies are a great way of showing this, of providing evidence of the excellence of your home; they can help to overcome common objections associated with 'being put in a care home', as well as removing the guilt that families often feel when taking this step.

Incidentally, we're in a touchy-feely industry, so don't call them case studies! It's best to use a term like 'Judy's story'. We love to read and listen to stories; however I'm not so sure we'd like our loved one to be the subject of a case study. It sounds a bit scientific and medical!

Professional and Government Standards; Profe
Associations You Belong To

In his excellent book, 'Influence: The Psychology of Persuasion', Professor Robert Cialdini describes how 'authority' can be used to persuade us to do things.

If you see a man dressed as a policeman, you'll naturally be inclined to do what he says. If you see a woman walking around a hospital in a white lab coat, carrying a clipboard and pen, you'll naturally assume she's a doctor and bow down to her superior medical knowledge.

The fact that the policeman is a strippergram, and the woman is conducting a poll of patients' opinions, is irrelevant. The uniforms they wear convey authority, and we're conditioned through centuries of civilisation to respect and obey authority figures.

I am a member of the Chartered Institute of Marketing. This is the most prestigious institution for marketers (not a high bar, I know, but nonetheless, it's not easy to get into). To become a member, you either have to take lots of degree-level courses with exams, or provide a huge amount of evidence and practical proof of your skills at a high level of marketing, as I had to.

I naturally, therefore, use my CIM membership to convey authority in my marketing materials. Similarly I have been a speaker at many of the national care conferences, so this is also used to add authority to my marketing materials.

This book you're reading now is yet more evidence of my expertise and authority. At least, I hope it is!

The same is true when it comes to your care home. You need to use everything you can that gives you an air of authority and expertise. Here are some examples:

- CQC Report
- Investors in People
- ISO 9000
- Food Hygiene Service
- Local Authority
- National Care Association
- The Social Care Commitment
- Having a key member of staff being a director or chair of an important organisation
- Being the author of a paper or publication on a care-related subject

Using the logos of organisations that have authority magically coats your marketing materials with *their* authority, competency, and legitimacy.

If you can combine this with key members of staff who are recognised experts in the care field, it will make it very hard for all the other care homes in your area to compete with you.

The more authority evidence you've got, the higher the mountain they need to climb just to get to your level.

Awards

In life, we all use shortcuts in our thoughts to guide us along. 'Expensive equals high quality' is a great example. If we had to evaluate every single circumstance we encounter through the day without shortcuts, life would grind to a halt.

Awards are another shortcut in our brain. If you won, or were even nominated for, an award, you must be good, right?

This is why things like www.carehomes.co.uk's Top 20 Awards, The Care Awards, or getting an outstanding CQC report should be shouted from the rooftops. If you have them, use them!

Photos, Videos and PR

Through your marketing materials, you're aiming to paint vivid pictures in the minds of your prospects showing how wonderful life will be for them, or their loved one, at your care home.

If you have a good care home, you'll provide activities, entertainment, and trips for your residents. You'll celebrate their birthdays, have strawberries and cream during Wimbledon fortnight, and wear fancy dress on Halloween.

Taking pictures and videos of these events, and writing a short description, is one of the easiest and best ways to provide overwhelming evidence of how great your care home is.

You can use it to influence not just potential residents and their families, but also social and healthcare professionals, the CQC inspector, and anyone else that's involved with/that influences people's decisions about which care homes to choose.

Pictures, videos and stories can also be sent to your local and regional press to create more publicity, which we'll deal with in more detail later in the book.

You may, by now, be wondering where and how you're going to use all this evidence you've amassed. So, let's take a look.

Spreading Your Message To The World

The next step is to take all your evidence and stick it in the eyeballs and ears of your jury (not literally, of course).

Here's how:

1. On your website

   Use logos of authority, testimonials, case studies, and anything else you can on your website.

2. On your blog

   Your website must have a blog, and you're going to publish everything on it.

   This is most important, as your prospect will study your website closely when deciding 'which care home should I choose for Mum?'

3. On your Facebook page

   Yes, I realise the thought of Facebook will fill some of you with dread, but like it or loathe it, it's where the eyes of many of your prospects are. It also plays an important role in Step 2 of the '3 Steps To Marketing Your Care Home', as you'll see later.

4. On your YouTube channel

   All your videos need to be posted on your YouTube channel, with links back to your website blog. This generates interest, and it's also good for Search Engine Optimisation (again, more of which later).

5. In the local and regional press

6. Across the rest of your social media

   Only do this when you've got the rest of it sorted - or have someone doing it for you (like us).

   The law of diminishing returns sets in once you've tackled Facebook and YouTube. You'll only need more social media channels if you have stiff competition, or you want to dominate your local market.

With the advent of the internet, increasing ease of website creation, and the introduction of social media, publishing content has never been easier - so make sure you use every weapon in your arsenal.

Repurposing Your Content

In order to get the most bang for your buck, you should use every item of evidence in as many ways as possible.

For example, a basic text article with pictures can be easily and quickly turned into a video and PDF. That means you can post it on your blog, your Facebook page, and your YouTube channel, to get maximum exposure.

There's another advantage that comes from repurposing your content and uploading it to multiple locations on the internet, and it relates to SEO.

If you include a hyperlink (the full http://www.yourdomainname.com) back to your website, it can help it rise up the search engine rankings. Also, your YouTube channel or Facebook page will be picked up by the search engines, and will appear when someone searches for your home online. This offers more ways for them to access the wealth of evidence you have.

Chapter 5

11 Touch Points And The Seven-Hour Rule

Buying something big or important is a bit like dating. No, really it is.

Quick confession here....

Having been rubbish at dating, and happily married for 31 years at the time of writing, I must admit that I'm using other people's experiences, together with my distant, hazy memory, for this analogy.

Anyway, here's what I mean.

When you're looking for someone to spend the rest of your life with, you don't propose after the first date. Falling in love may come quickly, and you may feel that they're 'the one', but most sane people take at least a few dates, and spend a fair bit of time together, before they pop the question.

It's the same for your prospective clients when they're trying to decide which care home is the best for their loved one, surely one of the most important decisions they'll ever make.

They're not going to simply choose the first one they come across. They'll do some research, establish their buying criteria, look for relevant care homes, and develop an emotional connection with the homes, to the extent that they come to feel they know, like and trust them.

In his book 'Oversubscribed' Daniel Priestley suggests this process of thinking, research and action for a major purchasing decision takes around seven hours; he calls it the 7-hour rule. I reckon that's about right for our industry, too.

The mighty Google has another way of looking at this. Rather than a specific amount of time, it uses what it calls Zero Moments of Truth (ZMOT). This is simply another name it uses for the various times a prospective buyer gathers information about you to help make their purchasing decision.

I prefer to call these ZMOTs 'touch points'. Google's research indicates that there are, on average, 11 of these for a major purchasing decision.

So what are the touch points?

They can be anything. Seeing an advert in the paper, driving past your care home and seeing the sign outside, talking with their GP or social worker, visiting your website, seeing your Facebook ad in their newsfeed, requesting a brochure, talking with you on the telephone, or visiting the home for a look around.

They all count, and the key to success is to make sure each time they encounter a touch point, it's presenting the right marketing messages. You also need to make sure you have enough of the right sort of marketing messages to fill the '7 hours'.

To quote Daniel Priestley again: 'You should have seven hours or eleven touches of relationship-building content at your disposal at any given time. Articles, podcasts, videos, apps, questionnaires, reports, illustrations, books, case studies and events – all of them count towards hitting the mark.'

The good news is you can take control of the touchpoints, to fast-track your customer towards a decision in your favour. You can also automate the process, using things like autoresponders and remarketing. More of that in section 3.

In the next chapter, we're going to look at where some of these touch points occur, and how to use them to eliminate your competition all-together.

Chapter 6

How To Attract The 95% Of Buyers Your Competitors Are Missing

All our employees work from home, as do I, so I rarely need a car. My wife drives to work, though, and she's run our trusty Jaguar for the last eight years.

However, over the last year or so, the service and repairs bills started to increase, so I began thinking about replacing it.

This started with day-dreaming about the type of car to get, what we need it for, and so on.

Next, I looked at motoring magazines, I watched reviews of cars on YouTube and, talked with family and friends about their cars, I mooched around car showrooms, downloaded brochures, and generally made a nuisance of myself.

I looked at purchase prices, discounts, the cost of keeping the Jaguar for another year, finance rates, PCPs, contract hire, lease purchase, and whether to run the car privately or through the company.

Finally, I decided on the type of car I wanted, and how I was going to pay for it. But that was far from the end of the matter. I still had to decide who was going to give me the best deal for my hard-earned cash before I actually made my purchase and got my hands on the vehicle.

All in all, this research and informed thinking took more than a year, but it was only right at the end, once I'd made my decision on exactly what to buy, that I was actually ready to purchase.

Just look at all those touch points, though!

The Buyer's Journey

My car-buying experience is an example of what is known as 'the buyer's journey'. Here are the typical stages (fig 5):

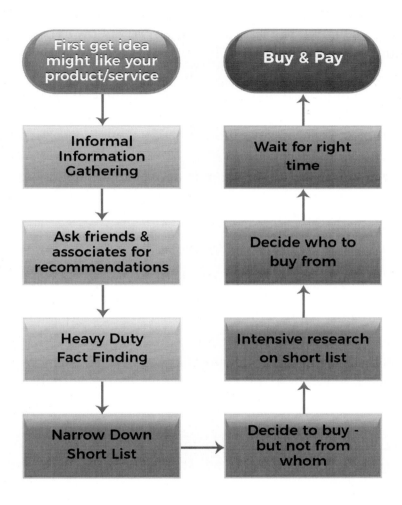

Fig.5 The buyer's journey

Now, let's group some of these stages together (as categorised by Richard Harshaw, in his excellent book, 'Monopolize Your Marketplace'), and I'll give you an example of how to use this to fill your care home beds.

At the start of the journey, you're at the 'Benefits of Ownership' stage. This is where you're searching for the best way to solve your problem or to achieve the result you want.

In the care industry, the problem is usually that the elderly person can no longer cope at home on their own, and their son or daughter is looking for the best way to get care for them full-time.

They'll search for information about live-in care, care villages, supported living, how the care home systems works, who's entitled to care, etc.

Next is the 'Objections To Ownership' stage. This is where they'll seek answers to their reservations about affordability, privacy, standards of care, and so on.

Finally, they'll decide that a care home is the best option. The question is which one to choose. This is known as the 'Vendor Selection' stage.

Most care home businesses (quite rightly) focus on finding people at this last stage - the 'now buyers', who are ready to make a decision right this minute. You should focus your efforts here first.

However, at any given time, only 1% to 5% of people in the market are actually ready to buy. This is represented by the purchasing pyramid.

The Purchasing Pyramid

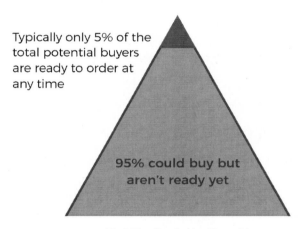

Typically only 5% of the total potential buyers are ready to order at any time

95% could buy but aren't ready yet

Fig.6 The Purchasing Pyramid

The hidden gold is in the other 95% who *could* buy but aren't ready just yet.

Find a way to identify them in the 'benefits to ownership' and 'objections to ownership' stages, and build a relationship with them so that they know, like and trust you. Then, when they get to the 'now buyer' stage, you'll be the logical and emotional choice. They'll come to you without even considering any other homes.

The way to do this is to turn the Purchasing Pyramid upside down, so that it becomes your marketing funnel.

Marketing Funnel

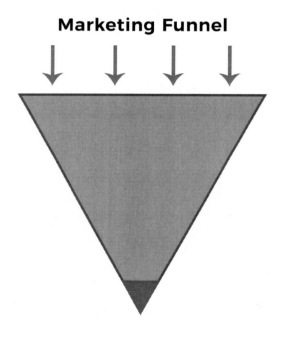

Fig.7 The Marketing Funnel

Remember Rose Lodge, the specialist dementia home?

Attracting the 95% is one of the techniques we used to help turn the business around. Since then, we've refined the process even further, using all the practical experience we've gained in helping numerous clients.

Here's what we did...

The Dementia Journey

People who are unfortunate enough to be diagnosed with dementia go through a journey with the disease, much like the buyer's journey.

At the outset, they aren't quite sure if they have it, so they'll start searching for things like: 'How to tell if you have dementia'.

Once they start living with the disease they find they need all sorts of additional information. What do they do about driving, for example? How do they make their home dementia-friendly?

As their condition deteriorates, their carer may need some support. Then they'll need home care. Next, daycare and respite care. Finally, it becomes so bad that they can no longer be looked after at home, and full-time care options are researched.

For Rose Lodge, we created a blog called 'Dementia Care Devon', which was linked to the home. On the blog we offered free reports that visitors could download, as well as lots of information that answered all their dementia-related questions. This helped create a relationship with Rose Lodge, and positioned the care home and it's staff as the dementia care experts for the whole county.

On the blog, Peter also publishes lots of evidence of the great job they do at the care home, just like we discussed in chapter 4.

In addition, Rose Lodge has many links to the community, and offers day care and respite care (when possible).

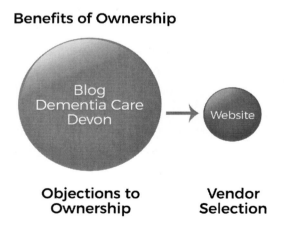

Benefits of Ownership

Objections to Ownership   **Vendor Selection**

Fig.8 Gravitational attraction

The blog acts like a huge planet whose gravity sucks in everyone in Devon at each touch point (when they're searching for dementia information or dementia care), and guides them inexorably to a place in the care home.

Firstly, by supporting them with useful information, then by introducing them to the actual care home and staff with day care.

By the time they need full-time care, the decision is made. They see Rose Lodge as the experts, and they've experienced the wonderful care the home provides and got to know the people involved. There's nowhere else they want to go; they're even prepared to wait for a place to become available.

That's the power of a fully-developed marketing funnel. It's the secret to scooping up the best prospects in your marketplace, and leaving your competition wondering how the heck you're so successful and never empty, whilst they're struggling to even get a glimpse of full occupancy.

We've now developed this technique even further, so that the whole relationship-building phase is done automatically, and without the practical involvement of the care home staff or owner. To do this, we use 'lead magnets'. Let's take a look at them.

Lead Magnets

Finding buyers for your care home is a bit like fishing. First, you need to find a pond with hungry fish. Then, you need to get some tasty bait, attach it to your rod, and dangle it in-front of the fish, to see if any are hungry enough to bite. The more rods with tasty bait you dangle in the pond, the greater the chances of snagging a fish.

The tasty bait for your prospective customers is a lead magnet. And, as with fishing, the more you dangle in-front of your prospects, the more likely it will be that you'll find new clients. You need at least one lead magnet for each stage of the customer journey.

Lead magnets are basically anything you can offer to your prospective client in exchange for their contact information, which you need in order to market to them.

By taking the lead magnet they are, in effect, putting their hand up to say they're interested.

To give you an idea of what lead magnets look like, let's use the lead magnets we use for our clients to attract people on the dementia journey, as an example. .

At the start is a free report called 'Dementia - How To Tell If You Have It And What To Do About It If You Do'

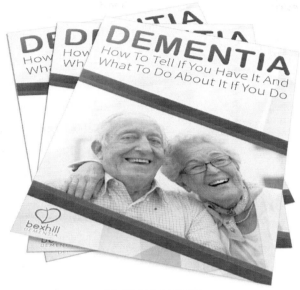

Fig.9 Lead magnet 1

This is obviously designed to be of interest to people who think they have dementia, but aren't yet sure. Here's a shot of what the report looks like. Notice that it's customised, in this case, with the Bexhill Dementia logo. The more specific you make your magnets to your audience the better your results will be; using the local town is one way of doing this.

Next, is another report called 'Living With Dementia', which is for the middle part of their journey. To capture people with this report you could use Google Adwords (more on this later) targeting phrases such as 'Can you drive with dementia?', or 'How do I make my home dementia-friendly?'.

You could also use Facebook Advertising to target people in your local area who have expressed an interest in dementia.

Fig.10 Lead magnet 2

Finally, when it becomes a struggle to manage at home, and they start looking at the next step, we have 'Dementia - What To Do When Caring At Home Is No Longer An Option'.

Dementia: What To Do When Caring Alone At Home Is No Longer An Option

This invaluable Free Guide will guide you through your options, including:

- Support in your home
- Community support groups
- Day care centres
- Short term respite care
- Full time residential care

Don't wait until a crisis happens. Download this Free Guide now and make sure you get the help you deserve and need.

bexhill
DEMENTIA

Fig.11 Lead magnet 3

When someone requests a report they must provide, at least, their name and email address. This gives us the opportunity to begin marketing to them. The object at this stage is to build up a relationship where they view you as the expert and begin to know, like and trust you.

To do this, there's a pre-written series of email messages that are delivered automatically, over anything up to a year, after the person first requests the report.

These contain lots of useful dementia information and tips. They also introduce the idea of day care, and the support group provided by the care home, which is the next step in developing the relationship, i.e. meeting them personally.

These particular lead magnets are in the form of a downloadable PDF. However, they can be made into printed material, audio CDs, or DVDs, as shown above. Physical items delivered to the person's home have a higher perceived value; generally, people are more willing to share more of their information to get these.

Obviously, they'll have to give you their address, and they'll probably be prepared to give you their phone number too. This increases the number of ways you can follow-up with them.

For our clients, we produce a branded DVD called 'How To Find The Perfect Care Home In…(the name of the local town). These are then offered on the client's website to interest someone who is actively looking for a care home.

Fig.12 DVD lead magnet sidebar graphic

With the technology available today, there are many ways that this can be displayed to the website visitor. They can pop up or slide in immediately when a visitor arrives on a specific page, appear after a set period (e.g. 5 seconds), or show when the visitor looks like they're leaving the page.

Sometimes, they are permanently displayed on the website - in the sidebar, for example, as illustrated by Fig.12.

In other cases, you may have a page on the website dedicated to the lead magnet. Another free report we produce for clients is designed to appeal to people who want to know about care fees and funding.

In this case, we're driving people searching for information about care funding and fees directly to this page. Here's what it looks like.

Fig.13 Opt-in page

Whichever option you choose, you need to have a mechanism for collecting the person's information; this is called an opt-in box. Let's take a look at your options for these.

The Power Of Micro-Commitments

An opt-in box, in its simplest form, needs to only contain the text that tells the person what to do, then two boxes - one for the email address, and one for the name. This is rather primitive, though; these days, it's much better to at least have an image of the lead magnet.

When someone clicks on the 'Download the Free Guide' button, shown on the previous image, the opt-in box opens and looks like this.

Fig.14 Opt-in form

Some people, once they see that they need to give their contact information, might abandon the process at this point.

To make this less likely you could use 'micro-commitments'. There is an immense amount of psychology behind this; if you want to dive deeper, I highly recommend reading 'Influence - The Psychology of Persuasion', by Dr. Robert Cialdini.

The short version is that we feel compelled to finish things we start. If you've ever watched a TV programme, or read a book, and not particularly enjoyed it, but got to the end anyway, you'll know what I mean.

When you combine this with a very easy, low-threat first step, it dramatically increases your chances of someone finishing the process.

In our example above, when someone clicks on the 'Send My Report' button, a box opens just the same. This time, though, it says 'Please tell us how you'd like to receive your report', with two buttons underneath; one saying 'By Post', the other saying 'Download Now'.

This is the micro-commitment. We haven't done anything scary, like asking for personal information, so it's much more likely that the person will take the next step and click one of the buttons.

If they click the 'Download Now' button they'll then see the opt-in above. If they click the 'By Post' option, the form would also include fields for their postal address.

It's also worth testing the addition of a telephone number box to each of the forms, but making its completion optional - to see if this affects the number of form completions.

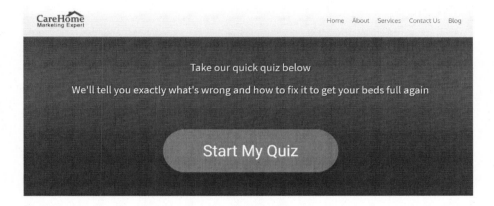

Fig.15 Quiz

An even more effective way of using micro-commitments is to reframe your lead magnet into a quiz or survey. This allows you to collect much more information about the person, and to personalise the follow up.

Fig.15 is an example we use on our own website.

www.carehomemarketingexpert.com/survey1/

This is cutting-edge stuff, because the technology for this has only recently become available, at the time of writing.

We'll be adding more examples of quizzes and surveys in the bonus content, which you can get here:

http://www.carehomemarketingbook.com/bonuses

Chapter 7

How To Fill Your Beds, Raise Your Prices And Create A Waiting List

Ladies and gentlemen, I present to you the Ferrari 'Laferrari'! Stupid name. Incredible car

Fig.16 Laferrari hypercar

When it went on sale, it cost a staggering £1,150,000. How on earth can any car be worth over a million pounds? And more to the point how come they could have sold out the entire production run several times over?

The answer is a perfect storm of ingredients.

Firstly, it's desirable. People *really* want one.

Secondly, it's scarce. Only 499 were made, and it sold out long before production even started.

Thirdly, it's exclusive. Before Ferrari would even consider letting you buy one, you not only had to have over a million pounds lying around in loose change, you also had to be a serial Ferrari-buyer.

What has this to do with filling care home beds?

Well, to fill your beds, keep them full, raise your prices, and have a waiting list, you have to create your own perfect storm with two essential ingredients:

- A highly desirable and unique product that they can only get from you

- Many more new enquiries than you can handle

It's simple supply and demand. If two people want the same thing, it's usually the one who's prepared to pay the most that gets it.

You have a limited number of beds, so when demand consistently outstrips supply, you can afford to raise your prices.

When you combine that with a highly desirable product that they can only get from you, people will *wait* to get a place in your home.

Let me be clear here. Not everyone will be able to, or want to, wait. However, you don't need everyone. You just need one person who is prepared to wait, and you have yourself a waiting list.

This is the key to long-term success and prosperity.

So, the question actually becomes: how do I create a highly desirable and unique product, and generate more enquiries than I can handle?

That is what I'm now going to reveal to you, with the '3 Simple Steps'.

PART 2

Step One - Strategy

Chapter 8

The 3 Simple Steps

You may recall the title, and therefore promise, of this book: 'Full Beds Forever - How To Market Your Care Home In 3 Simple Steps'.

Now's it's time to pull aside the cover, cut the ribbon, open the bottle of champagne, and carry out the grand unveiling, to reveal what those three steps are.

But before I do, a quick story… I know, I'm such a tease!

Why Shrek Is A Marketing Genius

The original Shrek movie is one of my favourite films. If you've seen it, you'll probably remember that, to get his swamp back, Shrek has to go on a quest to rescue Princess Fiona, ably assisted by Donkey.

The princess is being held in a castle that's protected by a dragon and surrounded by a moat of red hot molten lava.

The only way to get to the island is to cross a rickety rope bridge with rotten planks, which could collapse at any moment. One false step and that's it. Boom! They fall into the lava and they're toast. Very crispy toast.

This is exactly what happens when you try to attract new clients.

The bridge is the journey your prospective customers take. They approach the bridge the moment they wake up, as they think, 'Hmm, Mum can no longer cope on her own at home. I think we should start considering a care home for her.'

The journey ends when they've crossed the rickety bridge and reached your island, which is when they sign on the dotted line and become a full-time resident in your care home.

Each one of those planks represents a stage in that process. If your bridge is rickety, and made with rotten wooden planks, you risk them falling through and losing them, each and every step of the way.

Plank 1: If they do a Google search and your care home doesn't appear, that's it. They've fallen through, and you've lost your £78,000.

Plank 2: If your care home does appear, but they don't like your website and move on to your competitor's, another £78,000 bites the dust.

Plank 3: If they phone your home to make an enquiry and the phone isn't answered, or they don't like what the person says to them, or the person gives them incorrect information...again, that's your £78,000 lost forever.

Your job, as the person responsible for keeping the home full, is to make sure that all the planks on your bridge are absolutely safe and solid, so that at no point in that process will your customer fall through the cracks.

This is what marketing really is.

My job as a marketing expert is to show you how to do that, and that's exactly what the '3 Simple Steps' are all about.

The Care Home Marketing Expert Profit Pyramid

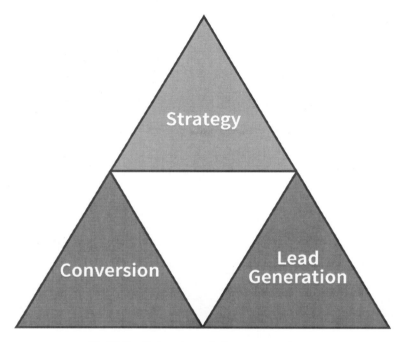

Fig.17 The 3 steps to marketing your care home

We call the 3 Steps the Profit Pyramid. They are:

Step 1 - <u>Strategic marketing</u> - This is basically what you say, who you say it to, and how you say it.

Step 2 - <u>Tactical marketing</u> - This is lead generation i.e. getting the phone to ring. This is what most people think marketing is.

Step 3 - Conversion - This is everything that happens after someone crosses the threshold of your home when they come to have a look around.

If you're currently suffering from occupancy problems, it will come down to a problem with one, or all, of these steps.

If the phone's stopped ringing and you're not getting any enquiries, the problem is likely to be with step 1 or 2.

If they come to look around but end up choosing a different home, the problem will be step 3.

Although I've listed them in this order, if you're going to build your marketing system from scratch, or you think the problem is a bit of each of the above, you need to fix things in the following order: 1, 3, 2.

Why?

You'll never get the phone to ring if your message doesn't catch your prospect's attention, engage them, and persuade them to take action.

Likewise, it's a complete waste to spend lots of cash, time and effort generating enquiries, and getting folks to come and look around the home, if they're not blown away by what they find and end up with your competitor.

Let's have a look at Step 1.

Chapter 9

Strategic Marketing

Fig.18 The 3 components of strategic marketing

Strategic marketing is what you're going to say, who you're going to say it to, and how you're going to say it.

Another way of expressing this is: having something good to say, saying it well, and saying it often.

The 'who you say it to' part is the **Target Market** section of our strategy profit pyramid. This means choosing the right sort of care to offer, and making sure there's a market for it in your locality.

The 'what you say' part is the **Innovation/USP** section of our strategy profit pyramid. It means innovating your business so that you have something good to say - something that's different, unique, and better than your competitors.

'How you say it' is the **Message** section of our Strategy profit pyramid. This means taking your USP and creating a message that's convincing and persuasive enough to get people to take action, whether that's ordering a brochure, calling you, or coming for a look around.

Targeting Your Market Like A Pro

Today's care marketplace is evolving rapidly, and your customers are likely to have a number of options available to them.

Home care, assisted living, care villages, combined with the rise in purely 'end of life' care, and dementia awareness, mean that the traditional residential care home is under pressure.

This is both a threat and an opportunity. If you're looking to enter the care market, it means there are more opportunities to satisfy changing demands.

If you already have a home and it's struggling (or even if it's not), you need to keep researching your locality to see what's changing.

Is the local authority putting more cash into home care to make budgets go further? Has a new home been built nearby? Are more people going into specialist dementia care rather than general residential?

If so, it may be time to change your business model to provide what people now want.

The key is to find the hungry market and feed it.

Now Is The Era Of The Specialist

Let's imagine you have unlimited funds and you're unfortunate enough to need brain surgery.

Who would you prefer to do the operation - a world renowned top neurosurgeon on Harley Street or the local general surgeon who also does vasectomies and removes tonsils?

If anyone's to open my skull and poke around in there I'd want the very best there is! And I'm sure you would too.

It's no different to someone searching for care for their loved one.

If your loved one had dementia, who would you like to care for them - the local 'old folks' home, who will take anyone with a pulse?

Or the purpose-designed, specialist dementia care home, with its expert staff, dementia-friendly environment, and endless patience and understanding?

Being the specialist puts you in demand, meaning you can charge higher fees, make more profit, and choose the customers who are the best fit for your home.

Take some time to review your situation and decide what you're going to specialise in.

Which market are you going to target? :- Luxury Private, Self Funders, Top-Ups, Dementia, Lifestyle Residential, General Residential, End of Life, Nursing, Local Authority Funded?

Before deciding, do your research. Look at the makeup of your catchment area. Are there enough high-income residents locally to support a luxury private care home, for example?

Speak with your local funding authorities. What sort of placement is there a shortage for? Are they struggling to find beds for high-dependency dementia care for those with disruptive behaviour that no one else can cope with?

Remember: 'find the hungry market and feed it'.

Chapter 10

Innovating To Stand Out From The Crowd

All care homes are pretty much the same aren't they?

No?

Well, take a look at most care home websites and advertising and you could be forgiven for thinking so.

Why?

Because everyone looks at what their competitors are doing and copies them. The trouble is, your competitors know nothing about marketing!

This means that all marketing materials look the same, sound the same, and they're all terrible. Let me explain.

Every market has *point of entry* features. These are the things that every business who wants to enter the market has to have.

Things like:

- Good food
- Dedicated, friendly, professional staff
- Comfortable rooms
- Staff industry training

- A homely atmosphere
- To be treated with care, dignity and respect
- Family-run
- Been in business since 1862
- Home from home
- High-quality care
- 24-hour care
- Activities
- Weekly GP visits

Any of these familiar? Perhaps you're using them too. Most care homes are, and that's why they all seem the same.

The trouble is, these are all things that *your potential customers expect all care homes to have*.

Fig.19 below is a recreation of a typical care home advertisement (we don't have permission to use the original).

There's nothing here to set this care home apart from any other home in the area. So how does the consumer choose one home over another?

The solution is to innovate your home so that it has some *point of difference*. We call this a Unique Selling Proposition (USP). It's also known as a Unique Selling Point.

Before you get all worried about trying to come up with something totally unique that no one has ever thought of in the history of the world, let me just say this.

Fig.19 Typical care home advertisement

You don't have to be different from every other care home in the country, just *the ones you're competing against locally*.

Here are a few examples of USPs that our clients have used very successfully.

1. Highest-rated (insert your category, e.g dementia) care home in (insert your town).

   This is based on your rating in www.carehome.co.uk

2. Winner of a www.carehome.co.uk top 20 award

3. Absolutely refuse to use agency staff

4. Guarantee that your loved one will never develop a pressure sore while in our care

5. The care home that local health care professionals choose for their own families

6. Unique location - e.g. on a sea front, or opposite a popular local park/beauty spot with a fabulous view

7. Unique building - a converted stately home or period building

8. Unique building or grounds feature e.g. koi carp pond with water fountain and sculpture

9. Unique guarantee - stay with us for a month, and if you don't like it for any reason and want to move, we'll give you a full, no-quibble refund

10. Staff call response time - under 2 minutes average, from bell press to appearance in resident's room, in a very large home

11. Staffing ratios higher than average/minimum required/competitors

12. Guarantee of continued place in the home, even if your private funding runs out

13. Awarded 'Outstanding' by CQC

14. Won local/national awards

15. The unique story or 'reason why' of the home-owner

For each of these it's not sufficient just to state it as I have above. You have to explain why it's important, and exactly how it will benefit your potential new customer.

That's the final part of section one. Next I'm going to show you how to take your USP to create strong and compelling messages.

Don't Be The Party Bore

There's always one, isn't there? The person who gets you in a corner and talks endlessly about themselves and their life.

REALLY BORING, aren't they?

The truth is we're not really interested in them and their life, we're really only interested in ourselves.

The same is true of your customers. They're not interested in you and your company, they're only interested in what you can do for them and how you can solve their problems.

When they visit your website looking for a suitable home for their loved one, they don't really want a care home. They want you to solve their problem.

They're desperately worried that Mum or Dad can't cope at home, and that they're likely to fall and break a hip or be sat there in a pool of their own urine because they can't get to the loo in time.

They're feeling desperately guilty because they can no longer help their loved one by themselves and they're going to have to 'put them in a home'.

They want you to alleviate their pain.

They want you to show them exactly how you're going to make these problems disappear. They want peace of mind and reassurance that yours is the best home where Mum or Dad is going to get the best quality of life.

If they get to your website and the first thing they see is 'Welcome to xyz care home. We are a family-run business that has been providing care in the home since 1922. We strive to treat all our residents with dignity and respect' Blah, blah, blah, blah, blah.....

That's the equivalent of being the party bore.

Only, this time, they can just hit the back button on their browser to escape from you. And that's exactly what they will do.

Chapter 11

How To Write A Sales Message That Compels Your Prospects To Desperately Want A Place In Your Home, *Even If* You Failed English And Can't Compose A Shopping List

Do you like the title above? It makes a big promise. Are you curious to know more?

How about if I'd used:

How To Write A Sales Message For A Care Home

It doesn't have anywhere near as much impact and appeal, does it?

How about if we change it to:

Discover The Little Known Secret Of Writing Compelling Sales Messages That Cause Your Prospects To Literally Crave A Place In Your Home And Totally Ignore Your Competitors

That's got even more bite!

How about another tweak…

Discover The Little Known Secret Of Writing Compelling Sales Messages That Will Have Your Prospects Literally Craving A Place In Your Home And Totally Ignoring Your Competitors

If you read that, wouldn't you just have to know what it is?

So why am I showing you this?

Well, as you've probably guessed by now, the words we use are <u>crucially important.</u> They cause us to want to get married, get divorced, start wars, give someone a hug, or punch them in the face.

The moment someone opens their mouth to speak you use their words to form an opinion of them. Often this happens very quickly with strong opinions formed within a few sentences.

And the same is true of the words you put out in your marketing. So, let's look at how to create a great message.

A.I.D.A The Key Formula To Message Success

This stands for:

Attention
Interest
Desire
Action

You can use it in all your marketing materials.

ATTENTION

The first thing you need to do is get someone's attention. This can be done with words or images.

The reason you see so many extraordinary images on television is simply to get your attention.

Talking frogs, dancing cats, scantily clad women. They're all there just to get you to look.

What about newspapers and magazines? They use pictures too, but they also use headlines. Here are some examples, with the motivation they're designed to evoke:

'London Bus Found on the Moon' - Curiosity

'7 Steps to a Sizzling Sex Life' - Desire

'Earn More By Doing Less' - Greed

'Do you make these embarrassing mistakes?' - Curiosity

How about some headlines that might grab attention for someone looking for a care home?

'The big lie hiding in your care home contract'

'Warning: Don't choose a care home until you read this'

'The new Boston care home that everyone's talking about'

'Why I put Mum in a care home (And maybe you should, too)'

'The biggest lie in the care industry'

'Why home care fails and care homes succeed'

'How to get outstanding care without breaking the bank'

'How to take the headache out of choosing a care home'

'Are you looking for an affordable care home in Luton?'

Now let's try combining a striking image and a headline. Take a look at fig.20 below.

Fig.20 Attention grabbing headline and image

Use an attention-grabbing image, headline, or both, and you've mastered step one and captured their attention. Now to step two.

INTEREST

Capturing attention takes only a matter of a second or so. Then the brain asks: 'Is this interesting?'

If not, and you don't follow your compelling headline with something that draws them in and persuades them it's worth reading on, you've had it.

One of the best ways to capture interest is to describe the problem that they're experiencing. It might be something like:

'Are you worried sick Mum's going to fall, break her hip, and be left in agony for hours before anyone knows? This happens to thousands of elderly people each year who live on their own.'

DESIRE

Now we've captured their interest by talking to them about their problem, it's time to introduce some desire. This is where you present your solution. For example:

'At The Pines care home Mum will be looked after 24 hours a day, 7 days a week. The home is specifically designed to aid those who have trouble walking and in her room Mum will have a call button right by her side so she can summon help whenever she needs it.

ACTION

Now you've got them on board, it's time to tell them exactly what you want them to do next. This is usually to call or visit, but it can be many other things, depending on what their problem is.

Here's an example:

'A fall can happen anytime. Don't risk it a moment longer. Call us now on 01977 232232 to arrange a personal guided tour, and for a confidential chat about your requirements'.

Let's combine all these elements to create a couple of adverts.

Do You *Really* Know How Mum Is?

Are you worried sick that Mum's going to fall, break her hip and be left in agony for hours before anyone knows?

A fall can happen anytime. Think how bad you'll feel it it's today.

This happens to thousands of elderly people each year who live on their own. Don't risk it a moment longer.

At The Pines care home Mum will be looked after 24 hours a day, 7 days a week.

The home is specifically designed to aid those who have trouble walking, and in her room Mum will have a call button right by her side to summon help whenever she needs it.

Imagine how great you'll feel knowing she's finally safe, secure and happy.

Call us now on **01977 232232** to arrange a personal guided tour and for a confidential chat about your requirements.

Visit **www.thepines.co.uk/dontfall** or **enquiries@thepines.co.uk**

Fig.21 - Good advertisement example one

Now, let's take one of those USPs we looked at before and use the AIDA formula to create a compelling advert.

Would you
want a stranger to see your mother naked?

Caring for your loved one at their most private and intimate times is a sensitive business. They want to be looked after by people they know, like & trust.

Almost all Leeds' care homes use unknown temporary agency staff. So your loved one would suffer the indignity and embarrassment of being dealt with by a complete stranger they've never met before.

At Nirvana Lodge we never use unknown or temporary agency staff. Your loved one will always be cared for by friendly and trusted face.

Why risk their happiness? Call us today to arrange a personal guided tour.

We'd love to meet you and the kettle's always on.

To discover 5 more unique ways they'll enjoy a better life at Nirvana Lodge, visit www.nirvana.co.uk/5-ways, call us on 01977 232232 or why not call in and see for yourself?

Fig.22 Good advertisement example two

See how that's so much more powerful, impactful and persuasive, than just listing the point of entry features like in the first ad we saw, in fig.19.

Summary

In step one, we looked at making sure there's a hungry market that you can feed; how you should innovate your business to provide something desirable and unique that your competitors don't have; and how to craft a compelling message to sell it, using the A.I.D.A. formula.

Time to move to step 2 - lead generation.

PART 3

Step 2 - Lead Generation

Chapter 12

Lead Generation

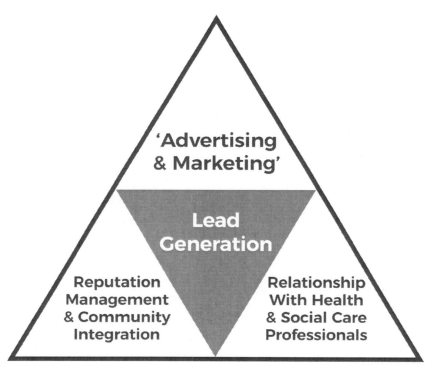

Fig.23 The lead generation profit pyramid

The lead generation profit pyramid

In the book 'Zen and the art of war', Sun Tzu says that 'Victory goes to the side with superior forces at the point of contact'.

This is a mantra you should live by in your marketing. In the first step I've just given you the tools you'll need to be the 'superior force' that will wipe out your wishy-washy, all-the-same competitors. Now we're going to look at the points of impact.

There are just four points of contact for a care home:

1. Online searches and advertising
2. Offline directories and advertising
3. Word of mouth
4. Drive by (nothing to do with shooting - they just drive past your care home)

I've condensed these into three main segments, which I've called 'the lead generation profit pyramid'.

The first of these is called **'Advertising & Marketing',** because it's what most people think of when you say 'marketing'. Really, this is paid advertising.

The second is **'Relationship with Social & Healthcare Professionals'**. This is pretty self-explanatory, but it's still a key part of lead generation, and how you approach it can make all the difference.

The third part is what I've termed **' Reputation Management & Community Integration'**. For most care homes, around 60% to 70% of their lead generation marketing efforts should be directed in this area.

Before we get into the meat of the lead generation section, there's one essential thing that every single care home business must have, regardless of how they generate leads.

What is it? Read on.

The One Essential Tool You MUST Have

The only lead generation tool you can't do without is a website. You MUST have one: it's essential, and it must be a good one.

Your website is like Spaghetti Junction. All roads lead to it, and it should smoothly guide your prospects to the next step of their journey with you, which is to come and view the home.

It's the first place someone will come to check you out if they hear about you offline, and the place they will ultimately land on if they come across you online.

Top 3 Website Mistakes

As it's so important, let's look at some of the worst website mistakes to make sure you avoid them.

1. It's all about you

   If you read most business websites they're all about the company and what they do. This is because, for most of us who have a business, we've risked everything to get it started, and blood, sweat and tears litter the path to its success.

   We love our businesses and we love talking about them.

   Unfortunately, our customers don't give a flying fig about us or our business - They only care about *what we can do for them.* So that's what your website should be about.

   This is why we spent so much time crafting your message in section one, which talks to them about their problems and how you can solve them better than anyone else.

Make sure you have professional sales copy written, that clearly conveys this on your website.

2. Amateur design work

   Would you buy a Virgin Atlantic flight if their website was a DIY job from 1&1, Yell.com or WIX or if their business email address was virginatlantic@yahoo.com?

   No, of course you wouldn't! Their credibility would be zero, because they'd look like a bunch of amateurs and you just wouldn't trust them.

   So why oh why, dear reader, do so many care home businesses think they can get away with doing this?

   Invest in professional design services if you want to look like a professional organisation. This is your shop window to the world that everyone will judge you by. Don't be a cheapskate.

3. Using a web design company to produce your website

   I know I just said invest in professional design services, but remember your website is a **marketing tool.** I can't stress this enough. Its primary purpose is not to look flashy. *Its job is to convert enquiries into people who come and actually visit the home for a tour.*

Web designers love to come up with gorgeous designs that have fancy sliding picture; massive, impressive-looking images that dominate the home page, and other such gimmicks.

These KILL conversions. Get a marketing company to create your website. They should have a good designer who produces a good-looking site, but it must be built around sound marketing principles, and incorporate the necessary marketing tools.

A blatant plug here. It will probably come as no surprise to you to learn that website building, along with everything else discussed in this book, is what we do for clients every day. So please contact us to discuss your marketing requirements.

In addition, our Full Beds Forever membership site (www.fullbedsforever.com) has a module explaining in great detail the elements needed to create a great care home website; it's well worth checking that out as well.

The Lead Tree

Back in the eighties, there was a very famous incident where Michael Fish, the weatherman, stopped mid-forecast, to say 'We've had a woman call the switchboard saying she's heard there's a hurricane on the way. Well, ha, ha, ha, don't worry, I can assure you, there's no hurricane coming.'

What happened next? You guessed it. That night, a hurricane hit Britain. It tore across the south-east of the country, flattening acres of woodland and trees, and leaving a trail of mass destruction in its wake. Seven Oaks was reduced to One Oak overnight, and Michael Fish was left with a LOT of egg on his face.

Why do I mention this?

Well, despite the massive destruction, there were still trees left standing that seemed immune to the terrible conditions. Why? Because they had strong, deep roots that the wind above ground could simply not overcome.

In business, I call this the 'Lead Tree'.

Fig.24 The lead tree

If you have just one method of lead generation, whether it's
your website appearing highly in Google search results, or a
good relationship with a social worker who steers all her cases
towards you, you're leaving yourself wide open to your lead
tree being flattened by the slightest breeze.

It only takes one change in Google's ranking algorithm to drop your website to page 4 of the results; or your social worker to move on, and you're up poo creek without a paddle.

Overnight, your leads will dry up. The phone will stop ringing and you'll be in serious trouble.

It's a dangerous and precarious position to be in.

I'm sure you can see that it's really important to build out your lead tree, so that you've got leads coming in from multiple sources. You want deep roots into the community, and to use lots and lots of different, paid advertising channels. The more roots you have on your lead tree, the stronger and more secure your business is going to be.

Now, before we move on to the actual methods of lead generation, let's look at another important aspect of ensuring your lead generation produces all the enquiries you need, just when you need them.

Chapter 13

Prospecting For Gold

On the 24th of January 1849, gold was discovered by James W Marshall, in a stream running through the hills of California. This sparked a treasure hunt, the likes of which had never been seen before. 300,000 people gave up their jobs and left their families for the promise of finding untold riches buried somewhere in the mountains.

How many of them came back with their dreams fulfilled? Hardly any. Most lost their lives in the pursuit, or died drunk and disillusioned in some gritty frontier town.

Gold is tremendously valuable, but the problem is it's also extremely rare, so you have to move mountains of earth or pan tonnes of river silt before you find any prized gold nuggets.

Imagine a lone prospector standing knee-deep in freezing river water, constantly sifting silt and mud at the bottom of the river. At any time, day or night, the longed-for flakes of gold might appear, carried by the current on their journey downstream. Alternatively, he may try and find the elusive spot where the gold flakes lay captured in the river silt, but which could be anywhere in many square miles of river bed.

The chances are pretty slim that he's going to find anything. Then, of course, he has to sleep, eat, go to the toilet, and fend off passing mountain lions; for these, he has to stop prospecting. That halves his already-slim chance of happening on his golden opportunity. His only strategy is to just hope he gets lucky.

There were a tiny minority who not only struck lucky, but also made large fortunes. So, what did they do different to the others?

In short, they were systematic and relentless. The smart operators got together, or hired prospectors, so they had shifts digging and sifting, 24/7, in multiple locations. This increased their chances thousand-fold and, provided they kept going and systematically covered all areas, it was only a matter of time before they struck gold.

So what, dear reader, does this have to do with marketing your care home?

The parallels between the two activities are striking. Firstly, each resident, like a gold nugget, is worth a lot of money to your business. If you're charging £500 per week, and they stay for three years, that person is worth £78,000 to you. That's the price of a near top-of-the-range Mercedes.

The trouble is, like gold nuggets, there aren't many of them. At any given time, in any given geographical area, there are very few people who are actively in the market for a place in a care home. The ones that are both interested and actually ready to go ahead are even rarer and harder to find. The chances of you simply happening across them are extremely low.

Like the successful prospectors, you need to set up your marketing to systematically and relentlessly find and connect with these people.

There is one crucial difference, though, which works dramatically in your favour. If you were a gold nugget back in 1878, you couldn't pick yourself up out of the river bed, go to Google, and search for people who can make you into gold jewellery.

Fortunately, your prospects can and do (search for care homes, I mean, not look for people to turn them into jewellery). We call this 'search marketing', and it's the first thing you should do to generate leads.

We'll look at search marketing in a few moments.

You shouldn't be content with just trying to find these people when they're actually searching. You should also find other places that have their attention, their eyes and ears, and say 'Hey! You know you're interested in a care home for Mum or

Dad? Well, we've got one that you'd be crazy not to come and take a look at.'

That's called 'interruption marketing', and we're going to take a close look at that shortly, too.

Just like the prospectors who got rich, the secret to success is to be systematic and relentless. This can be summed up in a **marketing equation**, which is:

Frequency x Impact = Leads

Frequency means you need to constantly be around. Then, when someone does start their search for a care home, they'll find you. You also need to constantly be in the places where these people's eyes and ears are, to prod them, and demand they listen to what you have to say.

However, it's no good just being there. You also need to have a strong and compelling message that moves them to take immediate action; to call you, or visit you. This is impact, and it's what we looked at in part 2, with the A.I.D.A. formula.

Do that, combine it with a great care home that people really want a place in, and you're well on your way to creating a waiting list and being able to raise prices, which is the real secret to long-term success in this industry.

Methods Of Lead Generation

There's no shortage of methods for generating leads.

Here's a list of some of them (in no particular order) that feature examples from all three sections of the lead generation profit pyramid:

- Website
- Search Engine Optimisation
- Google Business and Map listings
- Google Adwords
- Facebook Business Page
- Facebook paid ads
- Twitter
- Google Content network
- Re-marketing
- Business directories
- Care directories
- Local radio
- YouTube
- People travelling past the home
- Ads in e-zines
- Magazines
- LinkedIn
- Postcard mailings

- Leaflet drops
- Direct mail
- Banner Ads
- Telemarketing
- Press releases and PR
- Local trade exhibitions
- Free reports and white papers
- Giving talks and lectures
- Webinars
- Joint Ventures
- Affiliates
- Guest blogging
- Networking
- Local healthcare professionals
- Day care
- Home Care agencies
- Local Financial and Legal Advisors
- Respite Care
- Travel Agents
- Churches
- Ads in the Post Office
- Referrals from residents' friends and families
- Finders' Fee for staff
- Local Authorities
- Advertising hoardings (billboards)

I'm not going to go into *too* much detail, or even any at all, on how to use most of the above methods. Each of them is worth a mini course on their own; we've put together full training for each one in our Full Beds Forever Marketing Blueprint membership site. Visit www.fullbedsforever.com for more details.

That said, lead generation is vital, and I don't want to short change you, so we're going to look at some key methods of lead generation, and some crucial points that will help you be much more successful in your lead generation efforts.

And The Winner Of Best Lead Generation Method Goes To…

No one.

The truth is, ALL the methods listed work to some degree. The one you use depends on the type of client you want to attract and your local marketplace.

This is an important distinction in the type of lead generation methods; as mentioned earlier, there are two basic types of lead generation: search marketing and interruption marketing.

The Search Is On - Start Here First

Imagine how great it would be if you knew where the people who are searching for a care home in your town are - *right now* - and if you could put your home *right in front of them*.

Think that would get you more enquiries?

Of course it would! Now you can do just that, if you focus on search marketing. This marketing is customer instigated, and is therefore the most important type - because your potential customer is motivated enough to be actually looking for information or a supplier *right now*. They're therefore much more likely to be a serious buyer.

Before the internet, the only option your potential customer had was to consult the Yellow Pages or Thomson Local - the old paper directories that landed on your doorstep each year.

The advent of the internet, and search engines in particular, changed everything. Today, instead of you chasing the customer, they can chase you!

People still do turn to the Yellow Pages, but today it's Yell.com, or the Yell.com app on their smartphone, that they consult.

I'm not a big fan of Yell.com, as they tend to overcharge for what you get. However, the only way to know if Yell.com works for you is to try it and track the results.

I'll expand on exactly how to test and track a little later.

Search marketing is all about dominating the Google search results.

With Google, you now have almost the complete knowledge of the whole world and its history available to you through a small text entry box on your computer, tablet or phone. And it's free. FREE!

It's truly incredible. If you want to know something today you simply 'google it'. Want to know about all the care homes in your area? Just type in 'care homes in (insert your location)'. There they all are! Pages and pages of them.

If you want to find the 'now buyers', who want a care home *right now* for their loved one, and are searching for the best one, you need to make sure you show up in those results.

And you'd better make sure you're as close to the top of the page as possible. The higher up you are, the more enquiries you'll generate.

The only trouble is, it's not linear. 80% of the clicks come from the first 20% of homes shown. Therefore, it's hugely valuable to be included in that top 20%.

So, how do you do this?

Google Adwords

Fig.25 - Google Adwords' Ads on search results page

Let's look at a typical page of results (correct at the time of publishing. Google is evolving all the time, so this may change).

Google's results page is divided into three sections.

At the top are four paid adverts (see fig.25) that were shown when I searched for 'care homes in Leeds'.

These are called 'pay per click ads' (PPC). If done right, they're the most cost effective adverts on the planet, because *they only show up to people who are actively searching for what you supply, right now.*

And you only pay when someone sees your ad and clicks on it, which takes them directly to a page of your choosing on your website. Hence 'pay per click'.

Contrast that with a traditional ad in a newspaper. With that, you hope someone who's interested picks up the paper; you hope they turn to your page; you hope they see your ad, and then you hope they're interested enough to put the paper down and immediately go to their computer to find more info, or to write down your details for later.

The chances of all that happening are dramatically less - and you'll pay full price for the insertion of the advert, even if you get no enquiries!

Google's pay per click service is known as Google Adwords; it's the first thing we implement for our clients once they have a professional, high-converting website in place (from us, naturally!).

Google Business Page

Further down the page is a box that contains a map and three care homes.

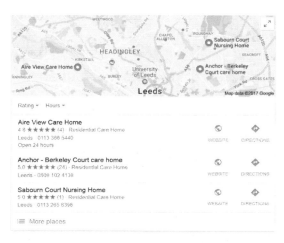

Fig.26 Google's 3 local business maps results

This is often known as the 'Snack Pack'. It essentially shows what Google thinks are the top three local businesses.

This area also gets lots of clicks, particularly when someone is searching on a smartphone. It contains a direct link to your own website, and it also links to your Google places page.

Google gives every business one of these local business pages that you can claim and manage (they're very generous). You can customise this page by adding your photos and videos, opening hours, special offers, etc.

This is also a place where people can review your business. It's no coincidence that Anchor's Berkley home at the top has 25 five-star reviews. Remember the power of proof and providing evidence from section one? Google thinks this is pretty important, too, and rewards those that provide it.

If your home isn't here, click on the 'more places' link at the bottom of the box, and it will show all the homes in the area. When you find your page, click on 'manage this listing' to claim and customise your page.

Google actually has a place where you can manage everything it provides for your business (i.e. places listing, maps, YouTube channel, G+) called Google My Business; I recommend creating a gmail account for your care home and using this for your Google My Business account. You can then manage all logins through one email address, and with the same username and password. Keeps life simple.

Search Engine Optimisation

Underneath the snack pack box are what's known as the 'Organic' search results. There are typically 8 to 10 of these. They are the other websites that Google thinks are the best match and most relevant to the term you've searched for (see fig.27).

For care home related searches www.carehome.co.uk usually occupies the top one to three places, depending on how competitive the search term is. That's why it pays to advertise there (see 'The Importance Of Proof' in section 1 for more info).

In this case, position two is occupied by www.carechoices.co.uk, while slot three goes to the Leeds government website, an on-line directory. It would be worth trying an advert in each of these, to see if they generate any enquiries for you.

Next, Anchor has two listings, both with star ratings shown. They've done a good job to get so high in the search results, to get two listings, and to get lots of reviews, so their stars are shown (these draw the eye to a listing, which results in more clicks).

To do this, Anchor have optimised their website for Google search. This is known as search engine optimisation, and is generally considered voodoo by most folks.

The truth is, no one really knows exactly how Google decides which websites are worthy and which are not; it constantly changes anyway, as they refine their systems and processes.

Care Homes Leeds Area - Carehome.co.uk
https://www.carehome.co.uk/care_search_results.cfm/searchunitary/Leeds ▼
Gledhow Christian Care Home. 145/147 **Brakenwood** Drive, **Gledhow**, Leeds **LS8 1SF**. Springfield
House Retirement Home. Springfield Avenue, Morley, Leeds **LS27 9PW**. Augustus Court Care Centre
Sabourn Court Care Home. The **Spinney**. Willow Bank Nursing Home. **Aberford** Hall Care Home. Oak
Tree **Lodge**.

Care Homes Leeds (West Yorkshire) - Carehome.co.uk
https://www.carehome.co.uk/care_search_results.cfm/searchtown/Leeds ▼
Visit carehome.co.uk to find **Care Homes in Leeds** (West Yorkshire) including The Spinney and Willow
Bank Nursing Home, carehome.co.uk is the definitive ...

Leeds City Council - Care Homes
https://www.carehome.co.uk/care_search_results.cfm/searchgroup/36154009LEEA ▼
Richmond House. Richmond Road, **Farsley**, **Pudsey LS28** 5ST. Dolphin Manor. Stone Brig Lane,
Rothwell, Leeds **LS26 0UD**. Middlecross. Simpson **Grove**, **Armley**, Leeds **LS12** 1QG. Siegen Manor.
Wesley Street, Morley, Leeds **LS27 9EE**. **Knowle Manor**. Tennyson Terrace, Morley, Leeds **LS27** 8QP.
Suffolk Court. Spring **Gardens**. The Green.

Care homes in Leeds | Care Services Directories | Care Choices
www.carechoices.co.uk › ... › Yorkshire And The Humber › West Yorkshire ▼
If you think you need help with social care in Leeds, read this directory for an ... Care providers and
care homes in Leeds – listed in the Leeds Care Homes and ...

Care homes and care homes with nursing - Leeds City Council
www.leeds.gov.uk › Home › Residents › Adult Social Care ▼
Residential **care homes** and nursing homes in Leeds.

Care Homes Leeds | Celebrating & Enjoying Life | Aire View
https://www.averyhealthcare.co.uk › Care Homes › West Yorkshire › Leeds ▼
★★★★★ Rating: 5 - 3 votes
Aire View is a respected residential & dementia care home in Kirkstall, **Leeds**. We are the proudest of
Leeds care homes.
Sat 5 Aug   Beach Party

Care Homes Leeds | Luxury Retirement Homes | Grove Park Care Home
https://www.averyhealthcare.co.uk › Care Homes › West Yorkshire › Leeds ▼
★★★★☆ Rating: 4.5 - 11 votes
Purchased in 2015 by Avery Healthcare, Grove Park **Care** Home is luxury residential care home that
offers independent retirement living
Sat 5 Aug   Beach Party

Leeds Residential care homes - Housing Care
www.housingcare.org › Housing & care homes › Residential care homes directory ▼
Leading directory of Residential **care homes in Leeds**, West Yorkshire, covering local areas Bradford,
Calderdale, Kirklees, Leeds, Wakefield.

Leeds Nursing homes - Housing Care
www.housingcare.org › ... › Nursing homes (care homes with nursing) directory ▼
Leading directory of Nursing **homes in Leeds**, West Yorkshire, covering local areas Bradford,
Calderdale, Kirklees, **Leeds**, Wakefield.

Corinthian House Care Home Leeds, West Yorkshire | MMCG
www.mmcgcarehomes.co.uk › Our Care Homes ▼
★★★★☆ Rating: 4.3 - 6 reviews
Corinthian House care home in **Leeds** offers great local amenities and excellent ... I then moved into the
private sector working in **care homes** where I ...

Fig.27 Google organic search results

123

The most important thing is to get your website created by a person who has an understanding of marketing and SEO. The coding that goes on behind the scenes is what Google's 'spider bot' reads. What you include here is your chance to tell Google what your website is about.

Some of it is also the snippet of text that appears on typical results listings, like those we've looked at. So, what you put in has to appeal to bots and humans alike, hence the need for marketing knowledge.

This brings us to another crucially important point.

There Are Many Parallel Universes Out There

At the very bottom of the page, on our search for 'care homes in Leeds', there a number of 'related searches' (see Fig.28).

Each one of these is a completely new parallel universe, that will probably contain a completely different set of search results, with new care homes, different directories, and a different results position for entries that make it onto both results pages.

Google relies on the single sentence, phrase, or word that you type into the search box, to try and determine exactly what you're after.

Searches related to care homes in leeds

leeds care homes **directory**

dementia care homes leeds

private care homes in leeds

nursing homes leeds **west yorkshire**

residential homes in leeds

care homes leeds **jobs**

leeds **city council** care homes

anchor berkeley court care **home** leeds

1 2 3 4 5 6 7 8 9 10   Next

Fig.28 Related search terms

The thing is, we all have our own way of speaking. We may use a variety of terms for the same product or service. Care homes, for example, used to be referred to as 'old folks' homes'.

This is less common in our politically-correct times, but older people, especially, may still use it.

People use the term 'care home' when they really need a nursing home, and vice-versa.

To get as many bites of the cherry as possible, your objective is to dominate the first page of Google search results - by using Adwords' ads, your Google places page, entries in online directories, and your own web properties - such as your website and YouTube videos.

The problem is, there are as many first pages of Google as there are different search terms that people use to find a care home, or specific type of care.

This is where you must be clear on exactly which terms, words or phrases (or keywords, as they're known) your potential customers most commonly use. Then, you can really focus on dominating the results pages for those searches.

This takes a bit of imagination, a lot of research (which we cover in our Full Beds Forever membership site at www.fullbedsforever.com), quite a bit of trial and error, and experience.

At least Google gives you a head start, by giving you what it thinks are the most closely-related terms at the bottom of the page.

That just about covers the places and tactics you'll need to generate enquiries from people who are actively searching for a care home.

But what about the 95% who are interested, but who aren't ready to buy just yet? Or, indeed, the 5% who are ready, but who aren't actually sat at their computer, doing a search, right now?

That brings us to *interruption marketing*.

Chapter 14

Hey, Stop What You're Doing And Look At Me, Now!

Have you ever been at work, concentrating hard - deeply engrossed in a task - when all of a sudden, there's an urgent ring, ring, ring from the phone?

You know this wonderful invention is a persistent little devil that won't stop until you pick it up and answer it, so you do. Besides, you think, *it must be something important if someone's ringing me.*

Only it isn't. It's some pesky salesperson trying to persuade you that they can save you money on your energy bills or your telephone.

It's *really* annoying, isn't it? This is interruption marketing at its worst.

The good news is, it's ineffective, so you don't have to sit there and work your way through the phone book, asking everyone who answers if they're ready for a bed in your care home! Apart from search marketing, virtually all other types of paid advertising and marketing fall into the interruption category (including telephone cold-calling, which is just plain bad manners and rude).

As the name suggests, with interruption marketing, you're trying to get someone's attention. You want them to stop what they're doing and to consume your marketing message, which could be some text, an image, audio, video, or any combination.

This is a lot harder than search marketing!

Time To Start Panning For Gold

Trying to find the 'now buyers', using interruption marketing, is a lot like trying to find 'gold in them there hills'.

When you find some, it's worth a fortune, but boy do you have to sift through tonnes of soil to get to those gold nuggets!

What you're trying to do with this type of advertising is deliver the right message, to the right person, at the right time, using the right medium.

The only problem is, you don't know who the person is, what time they'll be looking, or where they'll be.

The only approach that works is like the patient old prospector standing in the river. You have to systematically sift through the river silt, time and time again, until you strike gold.

For us, as advertisers, this means assembling a list of possible places to advertise then patiently testing each one several times, and with several ads, to see which produces the right result.

It could be any one of a number of different advertising channels; let's take a look at some of the more popular ones for the care home market.

Facebook Ads

We're going to look at Facebook business pages in an upcoming chapter, but for now, let's concentrate on their advertising platform.

Until 2015/16, Facebook had a relatively limited advertising platform that was best suited to big brands and large audiences. Local businesses didn't get a look in. All that's changed now and, unlike Google, Facebook knows a huge amount about us, from the information we give it and the way we use it.

This opens up a whole host of targeting options - a marketer's dream - that could dramatically improve our chances of finding gold.

Want to show your ad to people who have an interest in dementia? You can do that. Want to show your ad to people over 60 who live in your local area? You can do that. Want to show your ad to women over 60, who live in your local area, and have an interest in dementia? You can do that as well.

Narrowing your potential audience down like this means that you're at least prospecting in the right stream of the right river.

With advertising, the more closely you can match the advert's message to the audience who will see it, and the more closely that audience matches your ideal customer, the better response you'll get and the more enquiries you'll generate.

Facebook gives you the best chance of doing that.
Choose your targeting options very carefully, and create different ads for different groups of people.

A classic example of this would be splitting your ads between the elderly person looking for care for themselves/their spouse versus an ad for the adult child of an elderly parent, who is searching for care for that parent.

How you'd talk to each group, address their hopes and fears, and meet their objectives, would be completely different. That's why you need to make an ad that speaks directly to each one.

Also consider the objective of your ad. With Facebook, there are two possible objectives: making an offer, and building relationships. We'll cover the latter further on in this book.

When making an offer, we're looking for someone to take action right now (known as 'direct response marketing').

An example of this is offering respite care in the eight-week run up to the Easter holidays - a time when families typically want to go away, and need someone to look after their elderly relative.

To give this extra 'oomph', you might also do a BOGOF (buy one, get one free) offer on the respite care. So, for every day they book, you'll match it with a free day.

Now, I can hear you saying, 'What?! Give it away for *free*? Are you crazy?!' Well, yes I am. For two very good reasons. Firstly, *free* is the most powerful word in marketing. We all love to get something for free, so it gets results. Secondly, the real purpose of providing respite care is to identify a potential future full-time resident, and to start building a relationship with them.

Remember the buyer's journey in Chapter 6? Needing respite care is an important step in their journey with aging, which is likely to end with them being looked after, full-time, in a care home.

Intercept people at this stage, and build that all-important 'know, like and trust' relationship, and they won't even consider anyone else when the time comes for full-time care.

It's the same when offering day care. Elderly people perceive 'being put in a home' as 'a very bad thing' that they want to avoid for as long as possible. In fact, moving to a care home can actually improve their lives enormously, but that's not how they see it. Moving to full-time care is a big step fraught with danger, fear and mistrust.

Offering day care is a brilliant way of overcoming this. It gives the elderly person the opportunity to see, first-hand, what life in a care home would be like, without them having to make any commitment. This removes their fear.

Therefore, advertising day care on Facebook works really well, especially if you offer a free taster day. That lowers the resistance further, because they won't even have to stump up any cash.

It's also the sort of offer people will share, if they know someone else who might benefit.

With these sorts of things, the fortune is in the follow-up - so make sure you have a system in place for keeping in regular contact with the prospects you uncover through respite and day care. You need to continue that all-important relationship.

Anyway, back to Facebook ads. The final thing to remember with Facebook ads is that you need a bold, attention-grabbing image that's also relevant. You have to stand out in people's news feeds.

Fig.29 below is an example of an image we created for short term care over the Christmas period.

Fig.29 Respite care Facebook ad example

Another great way to do this is by using video. Facebook loves video, and their audience loves watching it, so you'll get high engagement and cheaper ad costs.

Print Advertising

Newspapers, magazines, and local publications have lost out massively to the internet, but they're still there. More importantly, they tend to be read by the older generation who are your decision-makers.

The same rules apply for advertising in print as they do when advertising anywhere else. I'm going to give you some important tips in the next chapter.

The main thing is finding the eyeballs of your prospective customers, which means identifying the publications they read. This could be anything published and distributed locally or regionally.

One of our clients in Yorkshire patiently took this approach and tested each local magazine, newspaper, local advertising rag, free paper and church magazine. They discovered the church magazine outperformed all the others combined!

That doesn't necessarily mean the same will be true for you. They were looking for private funders who wanted to make a lifestyle choice, not those forced into care by circumstance or failing health.

I would never have predicted that magazine would be the most successful, and neither would they. Anyone else who claims to know such things is leading you up the garden path. Only the market can tell you.

Popular Local Websites

Many popular printed publications will also have an online version, in an effort to maintain their readership.

Banner ads on these sites can work effectively to drive traffic to your website. These can be organised directly with the publication, or you can use the Google content network.

Remember Google Adwords from our chapter on search marketing? They also have an answer for the needs of the interruption market. They call it the 'Content Network'.

In this case, you create your ad, and Google will display it for you on millions of websites that carry content network ads. Your local paper's almost certainly has them.

Naturally, you don't want to pay for your ad to be shown across millions of irrelevant websites. So, Google lets you choose your targeting options here as well.

Re-marketing

Think of a time you've surfed the net and looked at buying a particular item, or gone to someone's website to check them out.

Then, as you've moved on to your favourite news site, have you ever noticed an ad for the very same thing you've just been looking at? What a coincidence!

Perhaps you then decide to pop on Facebook, and there's another of those ads. Strange... Next, you go to YouTube, and there's another! Now, that's spooky. And it happens again and again. Finally, your brain's screaming CONSPIRACY! *Are these guys spying on me, or what?*

You've just been remarketed. Amazon are masters of this, but it's really quite easy - you can do it, too. Why bother? In short, it's cheap, and rather effective.

Why?

For three very important reasons.

Reason 1.

It builds credibility, because it makes you look like a reassuringly large and successful company. When you're seeing those ads everywhere, you're subconsciously thinking 'Wow! These guys must be a big outfit to be advertising on all these sites.'

Reason 2.

It's cheap. You're only advertising to a very small number of people - the ones who've visited your website to check you out. You know they're interested, so it's almost as cost-effective as search marketing.

Reason 3.

You can move them along the sales process much more quickly.

Remember those touch points we were talking about earlier? On average, you need 11 of them for people to be comfortable enough to consider buying from you. Remarketing is a great way to shortcut your way to getting the 11.

Here's how.

Imagine someone comes to the page on your website that's all about your specialist dementia care. You've now got a pretty good idea they're interested in specialist dementia care.

Over the next two to three weeks you show them a series of ads.

- The first thanks them for visiting your website, and asks them to call you if they need any further info.

- The second is a video of a resident's family member, saying how their loved one's life has been dramatically transformed by moving into the home.

- The next takes them to your most popular blog post that shows the residents having a great time at the home or on a trip.

- The next sends them to a page on your website about prices (where you'll explain the assessment process, and invite them to call you to further discuss price ranges).

- The next asks your most frequently asked question and invites them to click for the answer (they are then taken to your FAQs page).

- Finally, you take them to a video of you, the home owner (or manager), talking about your goals and vision for the home, and inviting them to come for a personalised, guided tour.

How much more likely will it be that the person comes and visits after all that? Think what a different opinion they'll have about your home at the end of the campaign. You'll seem like a familiar, trusted friend. And, more to the point, your competitors will still be strangers (unless they're reading this too!).

I can't stress just how powerful this is when done right.

So, just how is this magic trick done? Do you need to be Penn and Teller to pull it off?

No. It's relatively simple to set up if you're into this web stuff (if not, talk to us). There are two main players in this field that you need to consider. One is Facebook; the other, Google.

They will both give you a thing called a pixel, which is a piece of code that you place on your website. When people visit your website, Facebook or Google notes where they go and which pages they view, before tracking them throughout their travels across the net.

They know where they are and show them the retargeted ads. Big Brother really is watching us!

Custom Audiences

Another great thing about Facebook and Google ads is the ability to create custom audiences. You can create specific audiences relevant to the page(s) visitors chose to read when they visited your site, and the actions they took when there.

This information can then be used to market to them in all sorts of ways, depending upon the purpose of the page.

Here are some examples:

- When someone visits a page about a specific type of care like dementia, general residential, dementia nursing, respite, day care, etc., you know they have an interest in that type of care.

  You could then do a follow-up re-marketing campaign specific to their particular area of interest.

- When someone visits the contact us page you can follow up with reminders of your contact details and offers of further help

- For special offer pages with an offer deadline, you could arrange follow-up re-marketing ads to remind people that time is running out, and that they need to take action before the deadline

- When someone visits your recruitment page you can follow up with current job offers

- If you have an area of your website specifically for social and healthcare professionals, you could let them know when room vacancies are available in the home.

The key to re-marketing (or any marketing campaign) is to be very specific about what you want to achieve. Segregate your audience to be closely aligned with their area of interest, then create a follow-up campaign that covers both the emotions they'll be feeling and the logical questions they will have.

Chapter 15

Drill These Into Your Brain When Advertising

Now that we've looked at some different advertising channels, here are some important points to remember that will stop you wasting your money.

1. It doesn't matter where you advertise, if you don't have a compelling message with a clear call to action your advert will fail. The message is crucial. Review section 1 for details.

2. The difference between a good ad and a bad ad can be the difference between one enquiry and six enquiries *for the same ad cost.*

    This is HUGE. This means you'll spend much less on your marketing to fill your beds. Or, you could continue to spend more, receive more enquiries than you can handle, create competition for the available beds, and subsequently raise your prices.

    Consistently having more enquiries than available beds is the only recipe for increased profits and

long-term stability and prosperity.

3. Spend your time creating several strong ads, then test them with multiple insertions in each channel before you decide something is a winner (or loser).

   That way, you'll find the ad that outperforms the rest, and the best place to show it. This is the 80/20 of advertising, and a massive growth lever in your business.

4. Placement of your ad matters. It needs to be read by your target audience, so choose a publication they read or a place they visit.

5. Unfortunately, no one really knows where their audience can be found. So, test, test, test. Test different publications and different mediums. You'll usually find one outperforms the rest by a large margin, but you'll only find it by testing.

6. Test small to start with, then roll things out on a larger scale when you find the winning combination of platform and advert.

7. Never pay full 'rate card' prices for print advertising. Always ask for a discount. Have an ad ready to go just before the insertion deadline - you'll get big discounts,

as the publication will need to fill space before it goes to print.

8. Always have a compelling reason for people to act NOW in your ad. An offer with a deadline works best for this. Also, use scarcity. You have a finite number of rooms in your home, so use this to create a fear of losing the room and not being able to get another one if they don't move quickly.

9. Always tell people exactly what you want them to do next. This is a 'call to action', and it needs to be clear, strong, and to move them to the next stage towards becoming a resident in your home.

If You Can't Measure It, You'll Go Broke

Along with many other witty and impossibly smart things, W Edward Deming is quoted as saying, 'In God we trust; all others bring data.' Nowhere is this more true than in marketing.

I once discovered that one of our new clients had been spending £200 to £500 per week advertising in the local newspaper. When I asked how many enquiries this had generated, they shrugged and said, 'I don't really know'. I asked how long this had been going on. 'About a year,' was the reply.

This was followed by a large thud and a long silence as I fell off my chair on the other end of the phone.

Let me be absolutely clear here. You MUST measure the return you get on every single penny you spend on your advertising and marketing. Otherwise, how on earth do you know if it's working or not?

Let's examine some of the ways you can track this, and how you define success.

1. Phone calls

   Someone phoning in with an enquiry about the home, as a result of an ad, or from one of your marketing channels, is definitely something you want to track.

   To do this, you need **Call Tracking**. If you've ever heard 'calls will be recorded for training and monitoring purposes' during a phone call, you'll know you've been call-tracked.

   Conversations are recorded, so that they can be played back to see how staff handle calls. It's not meant to be a witch hunt; praise them for what they do right, and give them training on what they can improve.

Call tracking also alerts you to missed calls, and gives you the telephone number of the caller. We install our own call-tracking system for our clients, and there have been several occasions where the home owner quickly called a person back when their enquiry wasn't initially answered by the home; as a result, they were able to convert some callers into new residents. The call tracking was therefore directly responsible for £78,000 worth of business that would have otherwise been lost to the competition in each case.

Another client identified a problem where the night staff were not answering calls during the evening. Again, sorting this problem out resulted in a much-improved service to existing families, and prevented missed opportunities like those above.

Call tracking works by using virtual numbers. There's no installation to do, and you don't need to change your usual phone number. These virtual numbers are just like your normal local number, except that they route the call through online software before it goes to the normal phone in the home, where it's answered just like any other call. The software does the call recording, logs the calling number, the time it comes in, the time it takes to answer, and also whether the call is answered or not.

Because the numbers are virtual, it means you can use different ones for different marketing channels. So, your website could have one number; your Facebook ads, a second one; and the advert you place in the local paper, a third.

Whichever number is dialled identifies the source of the call. That's how you track which marketing channel is responsible for creating that lead.

If you have a care home group there's an even more sophisticated type of call tracking, called 'dynamic call tracking', which you should use on your website. This shows each website visitor a unique telephone number, so when someone makes a call using that number, the software tracks where the visitor came from, where they go on your website, and even when they come back to your website in the future.

This enables you to hone in even more accurately on exactly what advertising or marketing channel is generating your enquiries.

2. Visits to the home

When someone walks through the door without an appointment, asking to look around the home, your staff

MUST ask them where they heard about the home. This needs to be built into their way of handling the show around, and we'll cover that in more detail in the final section: 'conversion'.

3. Actions on your website

Make sure your website has Google Analytics installed. With this you can track:

- How many visitors come to your website
- How long they spend there
- Which pages they visit
- Which website they came from
- If they came via a Google search
- If they came from your Google Adwords' Advertisements, and the search term that triggered the advert to be displayed

This is really important stuff. If you're paying YELL. com for advertising, how many visitors are they actually sending you, and how long are they spending on your website?

For example, they may send a lot of visitors, but if they only stay for a few seconds, you can be sure they're worthless as leads. Until you track this, you won't know whether you're wasting your money advertising with them or not.

You can also set up goals in Google Analytics. A typical goal might be visits to your 'contact us' page, contact form enquiries completed, or visits to a special offer page.

We discussed earlier how your website is by far the most important tool in your marketing arsenal. It's therefore important to make sure it's doing the best job possible for you. Google Analytics allows you to do just that.

There are other tools you can use to improve your website, though these tend to be for advanced marketers. We use software called Hotjar to record visitor behaviour. This gives us heat maps and click maps, so we can see what's engaging the website's visitors, and what is not.

For example, we tested the naming of the main menu link to the website page that carried photographs of the home; we used both 'Gallery' and 'Pictures'. It turned out that twice as many people visit the page when it's called 'Pictures' than when it's called 'Gallery'.

Since good pictures can have a strong influence when someone is choosing a care home, it's important to get as many people to visit this page as possible, so these things matter. And you only find out what works by testing it.

4. Codes, coupons and web pages

I'm an avid Radio Times reader. I like to plan my week's viewing, but I'm also fascinated by the advertising section at the back. It's a real marketing education.

It costs a lot to place an ad in a national magazine like the Radio Times. You can tell the companies who know what they're doing, because they advertise regularly and they use codes, coupons and specific web pages (and call tracking) to track responses.

When you fill in and post off a coupon for more information, or to place an order, that coupon has a code printed on it that's specific to that advert in that publication. When the coupons are received, the ad that generated it gets the credit. Similarly, there may be text that says: 'When calling, quote RT123 to receive your special offer'. Again, this is a reference to a specific advert that allows the advertiser to track the results it generates.

Finally, you may see the website address given as www.yourwebsite.com/RToffer. Any time anyone lands on this page you know they've come from your Radio Times' ad.

These are all things you can easily and cheaply use when advertising. If you don't, how can you possibly know if your advertising is working?

One final word on testing and tracking. Yes, it is essential to do it. It gives you the best chance possible of identifying what works and what doesn't, so you get your money's worth.

However, I want to tell you a little story.

My business partner's wife was looking for respite care for her dad while the family went on holiday. First, she called the local authority to get a list of homes in their local area. Next, she looked at the CQC reports of each home and discounted the ones that were below 'Good'. Then she visited the websites of the remaining homes to get a feel for which ones would be worth visiting.

One of the homes she recognised; it had featured in a couple of editions of the local advertising magazine posted through their front door every couple of months. She'd noticed the ads, because in the back of her mind she knew she'd be looking for a care home at some point.

After studying the websites, she decided on a shortlist of

homes. She called them to arrange an appointment and duly visited each one for a look round. Finally, she phoned the one she liked best to book the respite care. It was the home she'd seen in the ads.

This is a perfect illustration of the touch points involved in the decision to choose a care home. The question is, if you owned the home that was chosen, to which of the touch points would you attribute the sale in your testing and tracking?

You have to apply a degree of common sense. In this case, I believe the ads in the local magazine contributed to the end decision, even though they were not directly responsible for the enquiry. They made that home seem more familiar and trustworthy, which subtly made it stand out from the rest. So, while testing and tracking is important, like the Amazon ads that follow you around, so is being there all the time.

Chapter 16

Relationships With Health And Social Care Professionals

The care industry is unlike many other industries, in that health and social care professionals can have a significant influence on the decision of which care home someone chooses.

Because they visit the care homes they deal with, they get a good insight into what they're actually like - and they're unlikely to favour homes they have no confidence in.

They'll give the nod to homes they trust, and which they have a good relationship with, even though, officially, they're meant to remain neutral. Make sure that home is yours.

They also have increasing influence the more a resident depends on local or health authority funding.

Here are some tips on how to improve relationships with health and social care professionals:

1. Know who they are, collect their contact details, and add them to your contact database. Ask for a business card

when they visit.

2. Look at things from their point of view. They're responsible for the well-being of the people in their charge. If the care home neglects or abuses that person, it's their neck on the line. They'll be held responsible, even if it's not their fault.

   When you speak to them, always have their point of view in mind. Try and show how your home will help them to do a good job for the people in their charge.

3. Find and connect with them on social media, or have them connect with you.

4. Help them do their job. There's a great temptation to only contact them when you have a bed to fill. This is a mistake, as you'll be seen as the person who's always nagging at them and wanting something.

   Instead, take the time to think how you can help them. For example, social workers don't just deal with placing the elderly in care homes. They have a wide variety of people to look after. This makes keeping up with what's important in the elderly care sector very difficult.

   Be the one who filters out all the fluff, and who tells them, via your newsletter and social media posts, essential developments in law, treatment, regulation, etc. that they really need to know.

5. Treat them like your friends. Or better still, become friends.

   Send them thank you notes or cards when they're involved in referring a resident to you. Send them a card on their birthday or post on their Facebook page. Send them a note or card when they have a significant event in their lives that they tell you about - getting engaged, for example.

6. Give them feedback on the progress of their charges in your care. A phone call, email with photos or video of the person concerned, or a note, will be much appreciated and reassure them that they've made the right decision.

7. Mix up the method. Try to find and use their preferred means of keeping in touch, but not exclusively. Use the phone, in-person visits, email, social media, and the good old postal service.

This can all seem like a lot of work, and to be honest, it is. However, it can be significantly easier if you use a newsletter to convey information on a one-to-many basis. We're going to look at that in more detail in the next chapter.

Using software to deliver these means that they can be personalised automatically with the recipient's name and other details.

We use Active Campaign ourselves, and for our clients, as this has a lot of reporting and customisation options, but there are many others available for a very modest cost.

Another point to consider is: who's going to build and manage the relationships? There's a bit of a dilemma here for you, if you're a single care home owner. With a group, there's no choice but to let the care home manager be the one who builds these local relationships, albeit with the assistance of the group's marketing department, or folks like us.

If you own the care home, and are involved closely in the day to day running, I always recommend building the relationships yourself.

This way, when your manager leaves, they won't take the relationships with them to the next home they work for, leaving you to start again. This is also a good reason to keep a database, and to use software to deliver content that helps build relationships and to communicate.

This database of information then stays with you, and is even transferable in the event you sell the home, which adds to the value of the home as an asset (as does having a marketing system in place that consistently keeps your beds full).

Whatever method you choose, the most important thing is to keep in regular contact - to build relationships, and so you're always front of mind when someone is asked to recommend a care home (or if they're involved in referrals to care homes).

Chapter 17

Reputation Management

Despite all the fancy advertising we can do these days, word of mouth is still likely to bring you 60% to 70% of your new residents. So, relationships with health and social care professionals, actively building your reputation, and integration into the community, are where you should be directing most of your marketing efforts.

The one thing it's very hard to do is directly attribute your marketing efforts to success in this area. When you ask someone how they came to hear about the home and they say, 'I already knew about it', or 'so-and-so recommended it to me', you don't get the opportunity to speak with so-and-so, nor find out how they already knew about the home.

Unless they go past the home on a regular journey, it's highly likely they, and so-and-so, will know about it through one of the activities we're going to mention in this section.

The other thing to bear in mind is *what* they know about the home.

If they know of its existence merely from passing it on the way to work, their impression will depend entirely on what they see as they pass. So make sure what they see is immaculate.

If they've heard about the home from so-and-so, it depends on what so-and-so actually said, as to whether they come and visit the home or not.

This brings us to the important, but slightly confusing subject of your reputation.

6 Degrees Of Kevin Bacon

Have you ever played the parlour game '6 Degrees Of Kevin Bacon', where you challenge each other to find the shortest path between an arbitrary actor and the wonderfully prolific character actor Kevin Bacon? It's great fun, and based on the idea originally set out by Frigyes Karinthy in 1929, that all living things and everything else in the world are six, or fewer, steps away from each other.

What does this have to do with a care home's reputation?

When a home has a 'good reputation', you tend to think of that as a single entity. Your reputation is a thing that is built up over time, and it somehow 'exists' in the ether.

If fact, you have a different reputation with every single person who has ever come into contact with the home, or who knows anything about it, or even *heard* anything about it.

If you asked every single person you came across to rate the home on a scale of 1 to 10, you'd get a wide variety of different ratings. A disgruntled ex-employee might rate the home as 1, whereas the family of a resident may give it a 9, and a supplier may give it a 5.

An overall 'good' reputation is created when the majority of people, when asked to express an opinion, think that the home is good.

It's vitally important to realise that:

A) Your reputation spreads, using the six degrees of separation. It usually starts with one person's actual experience, but is spread thereafter multiple times as hearsay.

B) Each person's opinion is therefore not necessarily based on fact or personal experience. It's just something they think and say.

Your reputation is absolutely crucial when generating positive word of mouth, so the question becomes: how can you take control of how your reputation is shaped, to make sure it's good (or, preferably, outstanding)? That's what we're going to look at now.

Who Holds Your Reputation In Their Hands?

Just about everyone!

Let's look at a few key players in the reputation field.

Residents and their families. This is probably the most obvious one. Residents and families are the people actually using your service, so their word carries the most weight, especially with visiting health and social care professionals.

It's vitally important to maintain good lines of communication with residents and families. Really listen to what they say, as they're best placed to be able to tell you what needs improving in your home, and what you're doing well.

Give them a formal platform to provide feedback, and ask for it regularly. Speak with them informally when they visit - or all the time, in the case of the residents themselves. Act on what they say.

Hopefully, if you do this, and provide a great service, they will give you a thumbs-up when asked by friends and relations about your service.

Similarly, they will give you a great review when you ask them to provide feedback via review sites like Google Places, Facebook, and www.carehome.co.uk.

Ask yourself how you can provide the wow factor for them, by doing something above and beyond expectation.

One small example of this is to get some postcards printed, with the home's address and a nice picture. When a new resident moves in, give these to the family, so that they can let friends and the wider family know where Granny or Grandpa now lives.

Give them to the residents as well, so that they can let their friends and extended family know where they are. Help them to fill in and send the postcards. It won't cost a lot, but goodwill goes a long way.

Staff. Your staff affect your reputation in several crucial ways. First, the way they conduct themselves when delivering your service has an enormous bearing on what your residents, their families, and visitors, think of the home.

So, get them some customer service training. Make them understand the valuable part they have to play in the success of your business, and praise them when you catch them doing something right.

As Mary Kay Ash, the founder of the giant American cosmetics company used to say, 'We treat our people like royalty. If you honour and serve the people who work for you, they will honour and serve you.'

Above all, do what Mary Kay Ash did. One of her (many) other mottos was: 'I hire nice people. I don't hire people to be nice'. You can train people to do virtually anything, but you can't change their nature and character, so spend a lot of time and effort making sure you hire the right sort of people in the first place.

The second thing to realise about your staff is that they are ambassadors for your business all day, every day - including when they've left the premises. What they say to friends and family about your business, whether in person or via social media, all contributes to your reputation.

If they bad mouth your company, or any of your other staff, that can travel far and wide via the Kevin Bacon effect. And remember, most people's view of your home is based not on personal experience, but on this type of hearsay. Ensure your staff are aware that they are on duty, protecting your reputation, 24/7.

Suppliers. Many organisations treat suppliers almost with contempt. They view themselves as being superior to their suppliers, just because they're the customer.

What these organisation fail to realise is that their suppliers are also ambassadors for their reputation. They, too, strongly influence the Kevin Bacon effect.

How do you treat your suppliers? If you treat them poorly and are late paying your bills, you can be sure your suppliiers will be telling everyone just what a terrible business you are.

It's worth noting that negative feedback spreads 20 times more frequently than positive comment.

Anyone else who visits the home. This could be visiting health and social care professionals, delivery drivers, members of the clergy, visiting entertainers - literally anyone and everyone who visits the home.

There's an old saying that goes something like this: 'the way you do one thing is the way you do everything'. You can't change fundamental human nature. You can fake it for a while, but in the end, a person's true character will out. The same is true for company cultures.

So, make sure you, and your whole organisation, treats everyone with respect - the way you would want to be treated yourself. It's not only the right thing to do, it's also good business sense that will earn you a deservedly glowing reputation.

The Root Of A Good Reputation

As we said way back in Chapter 3, you can't make a silk purse out of a sow's ear. If your care home is a poor home you MUST address those issues first, and turn it into a good home before you start to spend money on marketing.

Let's assume that your care home is good. How do you take control and actively create a good reputation through the 6 degrees of separation?

It all comes back to the evidence we talked about in chapter 3. You need to show what a great life your residents enjoy at your home.

If you have a good care home this is easy. It's likely that almost every day there are funny, interesting, thought-provoking, touching, even heart-rending, things happening in your care home involving your residents and staff.

Your job is simply to record this kind of activity in pictures, audio or video, and distribute them to as many sources as possible. From now on, we're going to call the evidence you produce 'content'.

Here are some of the things you can capture to generate content:

1. Exercise sessions
2. Visiting entertainment
3. Celebrations, such as birthdays
4. Visiting animals
5. Trips out
6. New staff members joining
7. Staff members retiring
8. Charity and fundraising events, like Comic Relief and Children In Need
9. Pampering sessions, such as hairdressing and manicures
10. Special days, like American Independence Day; or Polish day, when you serve special meals, etc.
11. In-house talent shows, like Strictly Come Dancing or Britain's Got Talent
12. Special events, such as watching the Grand National, or the World Cup
13. Crafting
14. Playing games
15. Quizzes
16. Baking
17. Special occasions, like the opening of a new wing or room
18. VIP visits
19. Gardening
20. Tending to your animals
21. Afternoon cocktails

22. Your annual open day

This list could go on and on. All you need to do for most of them is to take some pictures and write a brief description of what's happening, and you'll have the content you need.

Another tip is to make someone on your staff responsible for collecting and publishing this content. Tell them why you want it, how often you want it to be produced (at least weekly), and ensure they have the tools to do the job.

I recommend getting a yearly planner. Work with your nominated member of staff to schedule some activity or event each week, so that you know they'll have regular material to publish.

In our book 'Practical PR For Your Care Home' we take this a step further, by providing a yearly events planner that's pre-filled with an event to celebrate every single week of the year. That's a whole year's worth of content sorted and ready to go.

Before we move on to what you should do with all this content, I want to get on my high horse again.

At the risk of offending readers, *I must stress* that the success you will see from publishing such content relies on you having a good care home in the first place; the type of home where residents are looked after properly, and where they truly enjoy a great life.

If your practice is to simply collect the cash then leave your residents half-comatose in front of the TV all day, every day, while their lives slowly ebb away, all you will generate is a deservedly poor reputation. None of the marketing in this book will help your business, if this is the case.

Sing It From The Roof Tops For All The World To Hear

Now you've got your content, what do you do with it?

Fortunately, with the advent of the internet, it's really easy to distribute your content far and wide, to be consumed by as many people as possible.

Fig.30 shows the main platforms available for publishing your content. These fall into two categories: those you control, and those you don't. Fortunately, even though you may not own the publishing platform, most of them fall into the first category, so you can decide exactly what you publish and when.

Fig.30 Content distribution channels

Let's take a brief look at each.

Facebook

Facebook is by far the most important place to post your content. You will need to create a business page that's properly optimised with the correct business information, and which has graphics that match your company's brand.

This is the place where you're going to build your community. Start by inviting the following to 'like' the page:

- All your family and friends
- All staff members
- All their family and friends
- Residents' families
- Residents themselves, if you have any silver surfers
- Your suppliers
- Health and social care professionals you have a good relationship with
- Visiting service providers, like hairdressers and chiropodists
- Visiting entertainers, or people who come to the home to provide things such as exercise classes

That should get you started with a good community. You need to keep adding to that community, and also use the Facebook page to generate new business.

Here's how you do that.

Set yourself a monthly amount for Facebook advertising from your marketing budget.

Spend 10% of that budget on 'Like' campaigns. This promotes the home's Facebook page by asking people to like it. As they do, they become a part of your community.

Spend 40% of the budget on 'content amplification', which is just a fancy way of saying: pay Facebook to show your posts to a wider audience.

It used to be that anyone who liked your page would automatically see your new posts in their news feed. Facebook has now got a bit smarter; plus, there's more competition to get into people's news feed; so, now you need to pay to make sure everyone who likes your page sees your content.

In addition to the people who like your page, you can also pay to have your content shown to other people.

These two segments are called 'custom audiences'. On Facebook, you can select a custom audience based on different criteria, such as age, location, gender, likes, etc.

Be careful to select your geographical location when you create an audience. Firstly, because your home is a local business, it will only be relevant to people in your local town, and secondly, you'll burn through your budget in a flash if you advertise to everyone in the country!

Spend 50% of your budget on lead generation. That's simply advertising your home and its services to try and find new customers. See Chapter 11 for details on creating great adverts that sell, and Chapter 14 for more advice on Facebook advertising.

Please note the above budget does not include the re-marketing recommended in Chapter 14. This is hugely important and worth its own budget.

YouTube

Create a YouTube channel, put your information on it, and add custom-branded graphics, as with the Facebook page. Make sure you include a link back to your website from the channel, as this is good for search engine optimisation (SEO).

Now, whenever you take a video of something happening at the home, make sure you post it to your YouTube channel. Also ensure that you give it a title relating to your business, so that someone searching on YouTube has a chance of finding it.

Next, add a brief description of what's in the video, and include the full URL of your website at the start of the description, as this is also good for SEO.

Other Social Media Channels

There are many more places, such as Twitter, Pinterest and Daily Motion, that you can post your content to. To be honest, I think the law of diminishing returns comes into play here.

There are advantages to be gained by using other channels, but it will not be worth your time to do it yourself. Unless you're going to employ the services of a company like ours to handle everything for you, I recommend limiting yourself to just Facebook and YouTube.

Website Blog

Your website should have a News/Blog section where you publish your content. We use the Wordpress Content Management System for the websites we build for our clients; this makes having the blog section, and using it, very easy.

Repurposing content on your website's blog that you've published on your Facebook page and YouTube channel provides indisputable proof of how good life is at the home.

This is important when people are on the website trying to decide if this is the right home for their loved one. It also reinforces the home's great reputation for everyone who reads your blog posts.

Email

You should create at least two separate lists of people to email. Firstly, the family and friends of residents. Secondly, health and social care professionals. You can then send different information to each list.

Health and social care professionals will be interested in information that relates to the world of social care and new legislation, as well as case studies and the transformations of residents who have come to your home.

Residents and families will be more interested in what's happening in the home, such as events, activities, and things like fee increases.

You *can* use something like Microsoft Outlook for emailing the people on these lists, but it's actually much easier if you use an email service like Aweber or Mailchimp.

These allow you to organise your contacts into subsections, and then to broadcast emails to everyone in whichever list you choose. More importantly, you can automatically personalise the emails, by adding in the organisation they work for, or the contact's first name, for example.

These two elements - using the person's name, and tailoring the content to what's likely to be of interest to them - will help to build up a great relationship with the people on the list so that, when asked, they recommend your home.

If you also choose to collect the names of prospective new customers - as we discussed in the section on lead magnets - these email delivery services will enable you to set up an automated email follow-up sequence.

For a single home, doing simple broadcast emails to the two lists, we recommend Mailchimp. At the time of writing, it allows you up to 2000 contacts, and the opportunity to send 12,000 emails per month - for free. It won't cost you anything.

If you have several homes, and are using lead magnets, we recommend Active Campaign. This is much more sophisticated. Going into detail about this service would pass beyond the scope of this book, but if you want to know more, you can always email me on hello@carehomemarketingbook.com

If all this seems a bit complicated, most marketing companies will be able to handle it for you; and that, of course, includes my team at Care Home Marketing Expert.

Newsletters

When you're producing content on a regular basis, it's a relatively simple job to put it all together in a single place, and make a monthly newsletter - which you can send by email, in the post, or both. You can also put a copy of the physical version in the information pack you give to people at the end of their show around. More of this in the next section.

It doesn't need to be fancy, and you don't need to be fabulously creative. If you're using any of the email services described in the last section they include professionally-designed newsletter templates you can simply drop your content into.

If you want to send out a printed version, that can be done simply and easily, too. Search for 'free newsletter templates in Microsoft Word' on Google, and download one of these that you like. Then, just like the email version, simply open these in Word, add your content, and print.

You can print them on your own printer, if you use thick, high quality paper and the highest print resolution setting. However, I recommend having your local printer produce them as full colour laser prints. If you have a group of homes and sending the same newsletter to everyone, it's worth getting it done professionally.

Whatever you do, though, please make sure it looks professional. Sending out an amateur-looking newsletter on cheap paper, with low-quality reproduction, will ruin your reputation rather than enhance it. As my father used to say, 'If a job's worth doing, it's worth doing well.'

Traditional Media

Every day, in homes across the country, editors of local newspapers wake up in a cold sweat, thinking, 'How the hell are we going to fill today's issue?!'

This is your secret weapon.

Build up relationships with your local newspapers. Provide them with interesting, 'feel good' content about your care home; offer to comment on the local impact of national social care stories and issues; write and submit interesting articles about social care issues...they'll love you forever.

You don't have to be Woodward and Bernstein. Local papers are full of simply written stories about moderately interesting local news. Rudyard Kipling used who, why, what, where, when and how - which he described as 'his six wise men', that taught him all he knew. If you answer each of those questions about your story you'll have it written before you know it.

Aim to get a new piece of content published every two months; this will massively increase your exposure via 6 degrees of separation. Just seeing your home regularly in the paper will make it seem familiar to its readers, even if they're not consciously aware of it.

And guess who they'll think of when the subject of care homes comes up?

You don't have to limit this strategy to local newspapers, either. Regional papers and local radio stations are also content hungry, especially when you have something newsworthy to report.

At the time of writing, one home wrote to George Clooney, who then made an unannounced visit to the home, much to the surprise and delight of the residents and staff.

As you can imagine, his visit was covered nationally, and created a tremendous buzz around the care home. Imagine collecting those clippings and then talking about it when someone enquires! And, of course, you'd have pictures of the event all over the walls of the home.

The daughter of one of my clients is a talented artist. She asked all the residents of the home to sit for her, and painted an individual picture of each one. The local art gallery then featured the entire collection, which garnered plenty of publicity in the press, as well as visitors to the gallery to view the exhibition.

All it takes is a little thought and creativity.

As an owner or manager, please don't feel you have to come up with everything yourself. Get your staff involved. They'll come up with all sorts of suggestions, and being involved is a great way to build team spirit and pride within the home.

Everything we've discussed in this section is really Public Relations, or PR. I deliberately haven't used that label, because I think it evokes negative emotions in many people, and it can make the whole process seem manipulative and false. It isn't.

Hopefully, you can see that it's simply doing interesting and fun things with your residents, to give them a great life, and then capturing it to share with other folks.

Chapter 18

Community Integration

If reputation management is all about communicating what happens inside your care home to the wider world, community integration is all about actually getting out there and building relationships.

These relationships fall broadly into two categories: those who can spread the word en masse via the 6 degrees (which usually means organisations), and those who can introduce you to prospective new customers directly, usually through Joint Ventures.

Joint Ventures. These are formalised partnerships where people who have the ear of your prospective customers introduce them to you, either on a paid, or non-paid, basis.

For example, people who are financially independent, and who can afford private care, tend to be the sort of people who rely on the advice of their solicitors, accountants and financial advisors.

Building joint ventures (JVs) with these trusted advisors can therefore be a great source of new leads, if you're trying to attract private fee-paying clients (and who isn't?!).

You can agree a fee with the JV for each person that's introduced, and who subsequently becomes a new resident. How much you are willing to pay will depend on your average lifetime client value, but it can be as much as £500 or more.

Alternatively, you can position yourself as the best provider for their clients, and help them to help *their* clients.

In either case, your job is to make it as easy as possible for the financial or legal professional to make the introduction. If you just ask them for referrals it won't work. You need to provide them with a professional referral pack.

This will include all the useful information their client might need to make a decision about a care home, plus the details of your home. This information should be co-branded, to emphasise the connection between the financial or legal professional and your home.

For example, we produce reports on how to find the perfect care home, and a raft of information about funding care home fees. Also included are details of the client's care home and what they provide, plus a special offer that's only for clients of the JV partner.

These can be printed, or in DVD format, and they're all branded with the logos and names of both our client's care home and the JV partner.

This looks very professional, and makes it really easy for the JV partner to provide great information to their client, and look good in the process. This means they'll be much more likely to do it, which means more success for you.

Incidentally, this referral pack can be used with any referring/JV partner, and doesn't have to be co-branded for everyone. Ask the local doctors' surgeries, chemists, churches, charities, WI groups, golf clubs, and anyone else you can think of, to display it for you in their premises, so that anyone who's interested can take a copy. To keep costs reasonable, this is best done using print rather than DVDs.

In the case of an organisation that has a membership structure, you can do a deal for the pack to be included in their monthly publications or newsletters.

In this case, it becomes a lead magnet. So they can get their hands on the information pack, you should direct people to an opt-in page on your website, so that you can collect their contact details and follow-up with them. Refer back to the lead magnet section for more details on how to do this.

Try to think laterally about who you could help by promoting your services. What about a poster in the window of the local travel agents, offering your respite service for people who want someone to look after their elderly loved one while they go on holiday, for example?

Spread the word en masse via the 6 degrees. This is a much more direct involvement with other organisations or groups in the community, and is primarily aimed at building relationships.

A typical example would be the local schools. My wife owns a children's nursery, and for many years, they would visit the local care home at Christmas to sing carols and perform their nativity for the residents, who all loved it.

The parents of the children were invited to come along - and many of them did, to see their treasured tots perform. Even the ones who couldn't come would see the pictures and videos on the nursery's website, and this, of course, became a source of proud (or, in some cases, embarrassed) chat with family, friends and other parents. There goes your 6 degrees again!

It doesn't have to be just the small children. One of our clients had the local sixth form choir perform at their home, which again, became the subject of many conversations at the school and the care home.

I have a dim, distant memory of visiting a local care home when in the sixth form; I played guitar while my friend sang. I seem to recall that we didn't always play and sing the same song at the same time! As in the Morecambe and Wise sketch, it was very much a case of 'I'm playing all the right notes, but not necessarily in the right order', which was a source of mirth for the residents, and substantial revenue for my future therapist!

The tables can, of course, be turned. You could give talks to schools and colleges about social care issues and careers. Many other groups, such as the WI, churches, charities, the British Legion, luncheon clubs, etc. are always on the lookout for speakers to give talks at their gatherings.

This can be a great platform for the 6-degrees effect, especially as the audiences often contain a lot of 35-60 year-old children of ageing parents, who are your ideal potential prospects.

Feeder Services

Home Care Providers. Remember the journey that people go on with old age? It starts with needing a little help from family and friends, and often ends up with full-time care in your care home.

In-between there's a stage where many people will require home care. If this is provided, or even supplemented by private companies, this can be another Joint Venture opportunity, and therefore an avenue for new leads.

Obviously, no home care company is going to give up their clients to you under normal circumstances. However, ultimately, many of their clients will end up needing full-time care. The home care company will lose their revenue when that happens, whether they like it or not.

What if you offered them a £500 golden handshake if they introduced their customer to your care home, and they subsequently become a new resident? They have nothing to lose, and there aren't many that can afford to say no to such an offer.

Day Care. The earlier you connect with someone on their journey through old age, and build a relationship with them, the better the chance they will become a new customer. So, why not have a day care service? Once someone comes to the home, experiences the high levels of care you offer, engages in the fun activities you provide, gets to know and like your staff and becomes part of your community, they are almost guaranteed to want a place in your home when the time comes. Your competitors won't even get a look in.

It's surprising how many people you can serve in this way. Let's say you have the capacity to provide day care to just two people each weekday. That's 10 places per week. If the average demand per person is once per fortnight, that means you can generate 20 new day care clients, each with the potential to become full-time.

Refer back to your calculation at the start of the book of how many new residents you'll need each year.

In our example, we had a 60-bed home that needed 20 new residents, per year, on average. A 60-bed home could probably provide day care to at least 5 people per day, which is 25 places per week.

How much easier do you think it would be to find those 20 new residents if you had 50 or 100 people using your day care service each year?

PART 4

Step 3 - Conversion

Chapter 19

Conversion

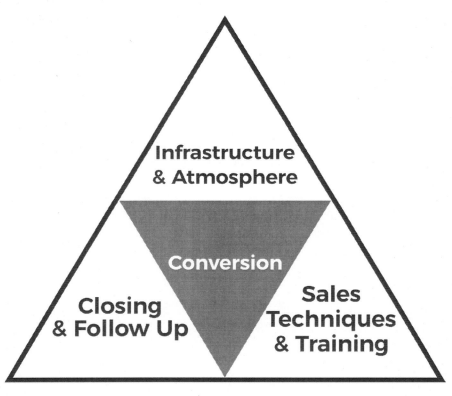

Fig.31 The conversion pyramid

The Conversion Profit Pyramid

So far, you've applied strategic marketing to create a compelling and persuasive message for your target market. Then, you set up numerous ways to generate new enquiries. The phone's started ringing again, and people are asking to look around your home. How do you handle it when they come?

Everything that happens, after someone picks up the phone to make an enquiry, or they cross the threshold of the care home to take a look around, comes under the Conversion Profit Pyramid and, as usual, it's split into three sections.

Let's take a look at section 1 - Infrastructure and Atmosphere.

Chapter 20

Cliché Alert - You Only Get One Chance To Make A First Impression

There's a good reason why clichés are so popular - they're usually true, and encapsulate a perfectly formed pearl of invaluable wisdom. This is certainly true of the popular phrase: 'you only get one chance to make a first impression'.

Everything we've done up to this point has been designed to create a picture of a wonderful care home, where every elderly person enjoys a pampered, cherished, and joy-filled life. So, when someone comes to look round, they'll obviously have very high expectations!

Your job is to ensure they're met.

The trouble is, it only takes one little thing to be wrong to cause doubt to cast its destructive shadow over everything and ruin your chances.

You see the conversation running in the visitor's head as they're approaching the home; it goes something like this...

'This place looks lovely! Mum's going to be so happy here. I'm so glad we found it.

Oh, wait a minute. The paint on that sign is peeling...that's not very good. And look, there are cigarette butts in the hedge bottom - that must be where the staff smoke. That looks awful.

Maybe this place isn't so good after all. If they can't be bothered to clear up their mess, or apply a lick of paint when it's needed, how bothered will they be about Mum's care? Perhaps this isn't the right place for Mum after all.'

To prevent this, everything your visitor sees and hears must be perfect from the moment they cross the threshold of your property.

- No peeling paint
- No overgrown, or weed-filled, gardens
- No litter
- No discarded cigarette butts
- No visible waste bins, or big, yellow medical waste containers
- No broken window panes in the greenhouse
- No confusion over where reception is or how to get in
- No miserable, scowling, grumpy staff giving your visitor the silent treatment

These are all things I've encountered when I've done mystery shopper exercises at care homes across the land. And it's not just outside the building.

I once visited a large country house that had been turned into a care home. It was a lovely building, set in a magnificent spot on one side of a large valley. On the other side, in the distance, was another country home, owned by Brian May of Queen.

The mystery shopper exercise was going well until we entered a dimly-lit, medium-sized room that was stacked with folded chairs and discarded wheelchairs.

In the corner of the room was an area with faded white tiles and a rudimentary sink with exposed plumbing. It was lit by bare bulbs dangling from the ceiling. Honestly, it looked like something out of a concentration camp.

The owner of the home proudly announced that this was the hairdressing room, where the ladies enjoyed having their hair done. Oh, and it was also used as a storeroom.

That was it. Sale killed, stone dead, right there and then.

<u>Everything</u> counts towards that first impression. If you muck it up, it's very hard to stop it colouring your visitor's judgement for the rest of their visit.

Get it right, however, and it builds on the visitor's already-positive impression, which you created with your marketing materials.

Have You Got Familiarity Blindness?

In our house, when my mother-in-law is due to visit, a state of emergency is declared. Everyone is on their best behaviour, and the house must be immaculate.

For me, a strange phenomenon occurs. I develop previously untapped superhero powers of observation, and can miraculously see hundreds of imperfections that just the day before, I'd swear weren't there.

A paint chip on the wall, a mark on the door, a small cobweb on the lampshade in the corner. Where the hell did they all come from?

Truth is, they've been there all along, but I'm so used to seeing them that they just disappear from view and I become blind to them.

The human brain has so many things to deal with in a day that it instantly decides whether something is worth our conscious attention or not.

To avoid overload, and to keep us safe, it only flags up things that are unusual or dangerous (like imperfections during a mother-in-law visit). That's why you can drive to work and not remember any of the journey. Nothing unusual is happening, so your brain soldiers on in the background and gets you there on autopilot.

This is a real problem if you work in your care home or visit it regularly. You become blind to its imperfections because you see it every day, but they stick out like a tracksuit at a wedding to anyone seeing the home for the first time.

And it's not just you. All your staff will suffer from the same familiarity blindness.

The solution is to have someone who doesn't know the home come in with a fresh pair of eyes and take a look around. You can ask a friend, or a professional mystery shopper, to do this for you. Either way, they'll be able to point out to you what's wrong and needs fixing.

If it's a professional mystery shopper they can do the whole tour and experience it exactly as your prospective clients will. They'll be able to give you relative, targeted feedback, concerning some of the important things we're about to cover next.

Setting up For Success

One of my favourite sayings came from a chap I dealt with when I was involved in the waste management industry. He was an ex-British army officer who was responsible for setting up the whole waste management system for Dubai when it began to explode with growth. Everything had to be perfect...or heads would roll.

He lived by the army's '5 Ps' motto: **Preparation and Planning Prevents Poor Performance**. Applying it is what got him through the Dubai contract, and he made it into a roaring success. Incidentally, his version had an extra 'P' in it, and was a bit more fruity, but I'll leave you to ponder that one yourself.

Fortunately, you have the opportunity to plan and prepare before your visitors arrive, so please adopt this mantra yourself and brand it onto your brain, as it's very important.

We've touched on making sure your infrastructure is immaculately presented in the previous section, but that's not the end of it.

If you've ever been to an expensive, upmarket hotel, you can't help but be blown away by the presentation of the bedrooms. The decor is subtle and reassuring. The bedding is thick, luxurious, expensive, and matches the rest of the decor in the room to perfection, as do the carpets.

The bathroom's fixtures and fittings are spotlessly clean, and work flawlessly, with a craftsman's precision. At the sink and shower you find branded soaps and shampoos in expensive-looking dispensers for your exclusive use.

The furniture is from a matching set, and feels solid and well made. There's tasteful artwork on the walls, and a beautifully presented chocolate on your pillow.

None of this happens by accident.

It's all subject to extensive preparation and planning. Every time a room becomes vacant, a well-oiled machine moves into gear, to transform it into this picture of perfection that's ready to sell itself to the next guest.

This is exactly what you must do in your care home. The moment a room becomes vacant, it must be inspected, and any and all imperfections fixed. Then it must be dressed to perfection, so it's ready to dazzle on the next showing.

To ensure this happens every time, to the same high standards, you must put systems and checklists in place, so that your staff know exactly what to do, and who is responsible for doing it.

Creating The Right Environment

Now the building looks a million dollars, the grounds are immaculate, and the room you want to sell is dressed to perfection, your first visitor arrives. What do you do next?

Well, what you absolutely don't do is immediately set off to show them round the home. You first need to put them at their ease and make them feel welcome.

Make sure that when they're met at the door, the staff have clear instructions to come straight to you, or the person who will be doing the show round, to let you know they've arrived.

And before your member of staff comes to get you, they should ask the visitor if they would like a tea, coffee, or glass of juice. They should also ask the visitor if they mind waiting whilst they fetch you, and that you'll only be a few moments.

Once you've introduced yourself to the visitor, take them to a quiet area where you can give them your undivided attention and have a chat without being interrupted.

This is crucial.

Once they're settled, and the proper introductions have been made, the real business of the show around can start. And that brings us to the next section of our conversion profit pyramid - sales techniques and training.

Chapter 21

This Gets Me So Angry

Remember way back at the start of this book, where we looked at the lifetime value of a resident? And we worked out that a new resident was worth £78,000 in our example care home.

That's a lot of money.

In fact, at the time of writing, you could buy a very nice new Mercedes S-Class, top-of-the-range saloon for that kind of cash.

Now imagine going into your local Mercedes' dealership to buy the car. It's an impressive-looking building: a showroom full of highly-polished cars that you can see your face in. Waiting to greet you is a well-dressed, polite receptionist, who calls you 'sir'.

You explain that you're interested in a new S-Class, so she picks up the phone, makes a call, and says someone will be with you shortly. She asks if you'd like a drink, then directs you to a comfy chair while you wait.

Fig.32 S Class Mercedes

All well and good.

Someone comes out to show you the car. But, wait a minute, he's not the sharp-suited, immaculately-dressed salesman you were expecting.

He is, in fact, a young, still-wet-behind-the-ears assistant from behind the desk in the parts department. He's nice enough, but he doesn't really know anything about the car. He just points to it and says, 'Here it is. Here's the interior. Here's the engine, and here's the boot. Is there anything else you need help with?'

You wonder what the hell's going on. Have Mercedes gone crazy?

Well, if they did that, the answer would be yes - they've gone crazy. They know they need a highly-trained, highly-paid salesperson with years of experience and product knowledge to be able to handle a sale worth £78,000. There's no way they'd trust it to the new starter in the parts department, any more than the receptionist or the cleaner.

Yet that's exactly what we routinely do in the care industry. We expect minimum-wage staff - whom we've employed because of their ability to provide care, but who have had no sales experience or training - to do the show around; our equivalent of selling an S-Class Mercedes.

And then we wonder why we have empty beds. It's complete madness.

The show around is the final £78,000 moment. It's what the time, energy and effort you've spent - creating the right strategy, and the generating of new leads - has been leading up to. It's what everything in this book has aimed at. Yet there's the very real risk you could drop the ball and lose the sale.

SO MAKE SURE ALL STAFF WHO MAY DO A SHOW AROUND ARE FULLY TRAINED ON HOW TO DO IT.

If you don't, it's grossly unfair on them, and you may as well burn your money.

Telling Is Not Selling

Phew! That was quite a rant!

Sorry about that. It just makes my blood boil. Hopefully, I've convinced you of the need to train every member of staff who carries out show arounds. Let's take a look at some of the essential elements of that training.

Most people think of a salesperson as someone who has the gift of the gab, and who can somehow smooth-talk you into buying anything, whether you need it or not.

Nothing could be further from the truth.

A true salesperson is more like a doctor. Before being able to prescribe medication or treatment, a doctor must first ask you specific questions to arrive at a diagnosis of your problem. Only then can they give you the right thing to fix it.

The same is true of the salesperson. Their real job is to find out what you want, and then show you how what they have to offer meets your requirements. And if it doesn't, or they don't feel you are the right fit to be dealing with their company, they must be honest and say so.

It's exactly the same when someone comes to look round your home.

You must skilfully ask them questions to find out exactly what their needs are; you have to listen very carefully to their answers, then demonstrate how your care home fulfils those needs, if indeed it does.

To do that, you need to know what questions to ask and the right way to ask them.

Let's look at questioning techniques first. There are basically two types of question: open and closed. Closed questions require only a yes/no response, while open questions encourage the listener to tell you more.

When selling, the majority of questions you ask are going to be open questions, so that you can gather information about the wants, needs, desires, hopes and fears of the person who's interested in care for their elderly loved one, or of the elderly loved one themselves.

Remember, you're trying to find out what the person really wants, so that you can hopefully match it to what you provide. An effective open question to ask, right at the start of the visit, is: 'Tell me, Mr Beck, what exactly has prompted you to come and visit the care home today?'

What you're looking for is the exact event that moved them from just considering a care home to actually looking for one immediately.

It may be that Mum has fallen, but not been seriously injured, but it's resulted in the family not daring to leave her on her own anymore.

If that were the case, you'd stress, during the show around, that she will be cared for and monitored 24/7, so that if she fell again, she'd receive immediate assistance, and not be left for hours on the floor, in agony with a broken hip.

Another question to ask is: 'How would you describe your mum's personality?'

Here, we're looking for her likes and dislikes.

You would also use closed questions at this early stage of the visit, to find out specific things. For example: 'Are you looking for full-time care for Mum?'

Remember, we're still in our quiet area at this point, and you're trying to get to know the visitor, their elderly loved one, and their situation. It's easy for this to seem like an interrogation if you keep firing questions at the person, particularly closed questions.

Your visitor is likely to be quite nervous, so be friendly; use lots of open questions to get them talking, and LISTEN carefully to the answers. Do not interrupt, even if you've heard the answers you're getting many times before.

The title of this chapter is 'Telling Is Not Selling'. The worst mistake I see care home staff make during a show around is to sit the visitor down and begin to tell them all about the care home before the visitor has even had a chance to speak.

Remember, the show around is about them, not you. You're trying to find out what their specific requirements are, so that you can show them just how your care home matches them. To do that, you need to be listening at least twice as much as you're talking.

Only when you've gathered as much information as you can is it time to move on to actually showing the person around the home.

Next, I'm going to show you how to use the information you've gathered to sell the home.

Come And See What We've Got

Now you're in the driving seat, and taking the visitor on a tour of the home. You want to sell the home to them, but how do you go about it?

You're going to use F.A.B. That stands for Features, Advantages, Benefits.

Let me give you a couple of examples to illustrate.

You're going to a party and you want to buy a new dress. The sales assistant suggests a red dress (that's the Feature). She goes on to explain how red really suits your colouring (that's the advantage). Next, she says, 'Just imagine how great you'll feel with all the chaps at the party looking at you, thinking how fabulous you look in your new red dress.' (That's the benefit.)

If the sales assistant had just said, 'Try the red dress', without explaining any advantages and benefits (there are usually more than one of each), it would be much less persuasive.

You'd be left to make the rest up yourself, and we all know what happens then. Your brain kicks in and starts making you doubt everything. 'Does it make me look fat? Does it suit me? Maybe red's a bit too tarty. etc.'

Let's take another example. You need to buy a new 4mm drill bit for your drill, to put up some shelves in the house. Actually, what you really want is not a 4mm drill bit (the feature); you want a hole (the advantage), because that will enable you to put up the shelves and stop your partner from nagging you about it (the benefit). She says, 'you bought the damned things six months ago, and they've been sat there waiting for you to put them up ever since!'

When you buy your 4mm drill bit, you're really buying peace of mind.

Let's explore an example that uses the information you've just gathered, about the elderly loved one of the person you're showing around the home. You discovered that Mum is a bit anti-social; she prefers her own company and likes to read quietly.

So you show them the quiet corner (feature), where Mum can sit peacefully enjoying her own company while she reads one of the many books you have in your library (advantage). Then you say, 'It'll be great to know that Mum will still be able to enjoy the things that make her happy when she moves in, won't it?' (a benefit to both Mum and to the son/daughter).

Now imagine what would have happened if you hadn't taken the time to find out about Mum with your initial open questions. You could have just gone round and showed the visitor all the fun and engaging activities that Mum can get involved in, and stressed what a great community you have, where everyone gets together and becomes friends.

If you'd done that, your visitor would be smiling politely while all the time thinking, 'Mum would absolutely hate it here. She just wants to be left alone to do her own thing, and now she's going to be dragged into all these activities with people she doesn't even know.' And that would be that - the sale lost.

Remember, the job of a salesperson is to discover what the person wants, and to show how their offering provides it.

It's Great, But… Handling Objections

Objections are things in the buyer's mind that you'll need to overcome, in order to make the sale and convert your visitor, or their elderly loved one, into a new resident for the home. There may be some things in your home that you know are at a disadvantage, compared to your competition, or compared to the expectations of the person you're showing around.

A typical example of this would be not having an en-suite bathroom. Most sons and daughters of ageing parents are used to having an en-suite at home, and when they use a hotel, so they'll expect your care home to have them, too.

If you don't have a room with an en-suite available, the question you should ask when you're in the room is: 'How important do you think an en-suite will be to your mum?'

It's important to ask the question about the potential resident, rather than the son or daughter, because it forces them to consider things from the parent's point of view.

Until you ask the question, you don't know what's going on in the mind of the person you're showing around. It may be that Mum doesn't have an en-suite at home; in that case, it won't be an issue.

It may be that an en-suite is really important, and a potential deal breaker. Or it may be that the son or daughter doesn't want to pay for an en-suite room, because the extra cost will eat into their potential inheritance. You just don't know until you ask.

To handle an objection such as this, I recommend using the Feel, Felt, Found method. This is where you say, 'I understand why you would *feel* that way', then you give an example of someone else who *felt* the same concern. Finally, you go on to explain that they *found* it wasn't an issue, and give the reason.

For the en-suite objection you might say, 'I understand why you *feel* an en-suite is important. In fact, Mrs Elsie Smith, who moved here a few weeks ago, *felt* exactly the same way. However, we put a commode right next to her bed, and she *found* that it was actually more convenient than her groping her way across the room to the bathroom in the dark, and negated the risk of her falling.

She was on the list to move to a room with an en-suite as soon as one became available, but now it's no longer an issue, and she's really happy with the room she has.'

To find out about other potential objections, you must listen very carefully to the questions people ask you as you go around the home.

For example, someone may ask, 'Do you have a lift?' It would be very easy to answer yes or no to this question, but if you did, you wouldn't discover the reason the person asked the question, which could be a potential objection you'll need to overcome.

So, when you get asked a question like this, use the elastic band technique, and ping it right back at them with another question, to uncover what's behind their query.

In this case, you might say, 'Is having a lift important to you?' They will then tell you why - or they may just say yes, in which case, you must ask them why.

Let's say they answer, 'Yes, Mum has a real fear of falling on the stairs, so she wants a place that has a lift, or a downstairs room.'

You now have a number of choices:

1. Offer a downstairs room, if you have one available
2. Explain that you do have a lift
3. If you don't have a lift, or a downstairs room, explain that she need only press the buzzer and a member of staff will guide her down the stairs every time, so there's no chance of her falling

Whichever one you choose, you must discover whether that has fully answered the objection. Say, 'Is that OK?'

They will either say yes, or go on to describe any lingering concerns. It's important to get to the bottom of objections and handle them effectively before we move on to the next section, which is closing and follow-up.

Let's take a look at that now.

Chapter 22

The Dreaded Close

Ok, now you've done the show around; you've shown all the features that match what the visitor wants and needs, and dealt with any objections.

Now it's time to wrap things up and try to get a commitment.

To do this, take the person back to the quiet place and review the visit. List all the features you pointed out and reiterate the advantages and benefits of each. Then ask the £78,000 question. 'From what you've seen, do you think this is the right home for Mum?'

What happens next is really important. Shut up until you get a reply. After you've asked what may seem an uncomfortably direct question, each moment of ensuing silence can seem like an eternity, and it's common to want to jump in and fill it with something.

Don't. Under any circumstances.

If the person says yes, then move into the assumptive close. Say something like, 'Great! We'll reserve the room for...' Or, 'The next step is...'

Go on to describe the next steps. Ask for a date when they'd like Mum to move in.

I realise that it's not always possible for people to make a decision there and then. Often, social services are involved, and more things need to be sorted before a definite yes can be given. What you're aiming for is a rock-solid, positive commitment for the next step, preferably with an agreed date as to when it will happen.

The next step might be to do an assessment, or a date for the potential resident to come and see the home for themselves - so they can spend a day, or longer, with you, to make sure they like it.

Whatever gets a commitment, and moves you to the next stage with a definite date (preferably one that's written in the diary) is good.

It's highly unlikely you'll get a straight 'no' to your closing question. If you do, that's good in a way, because it saves a lot of wasted time following up with someone who's never going to say yes.

But, often, you won't get a straight yes. This means one of two things: either there's something holding them back that you haven't yet discovered, or they've decided against your home and they're too polite to tell you so.

At this point, you need to do some digging. Go over the requirements they gave you at the initial questioning stage; review how the home meets those requirements, then ask, 'Is there anything else stopping you going ahead that we haven't covered?'

They'll either tell you the real objection, or they'll stall even further. If the objection is revealed, don't answer it immediately. Instead, say, 'Apart from (whatever the objection is), is there anything else that concerns you that we haven't covered?'

If they say no, go ahead and answer the objection, then ask for their commitment to the next step as before. If they say yes, let them outline the objection then ask again: 'Apart from (whatever the objection is), is there anything else that concerns you that we haven't covered?'

If they say no, go for the commitment. If they say yes, ask, 'Apart from (whatever the objection is), is there anything else that concerns you that we haven't covered?' Continue until there are no more objections left.

List their objections. Go through them one by one, and at the end of each, ask them if that has answered their query satisfactorily. If not, go back until you have. Then move to the next objection and do the same again. Do this for each and every objection.

When you've done, summarise the objections and your answer to each, then ask the closing question again: 'Apart from (whatever the objection is), is there anything else that concerns you that we haven't covered?'

At this point, if they still avoid making a commitment, it's likely that they're just wasting your time, so wrap it up - or, if you're feeling brave, ask them straight out if they're actually interested or not.

Hopefully, after all that, you can dismiss your visitor as a potential new customer; or, you'll have the next step determined, a commitment, and a time agreed for when it should happen.

If it's the latter, it's still important to follow-up with them. We'll cover that in the next step.

The Fortune's In The Follow-Up

I was going to use 'Follow Up Until They Buy Or Die' - a great sales industry mantra - for this chapter title.

However, that might be somewhat insensitive for an industry concerned with caring for the elderly! So, 'The Fortune's In The Follow-Up' it is.

The meaning of each is the same, though. Once your visitor has left the building, your job is far from over. There's many a slip 'twixt the cup and the lip, as the saying goes; you can't count the person as a new resident until they've signed a contract and moved in.

So, what else can you do to improve your chances of that happening?

Well, let's go back a step first.

Throughout the marketing you create, and the service you provide, try and stand out from your competitors for the right reasons, by providing exceptional service and facilities that make them go 'WOW'!

I know that it's easier said than done. Having the question in your mind, 'How can I give this the WOW factor?', will give you a fighting chance, and you'll be surprised at what you can come up with.

For following up, there are three ways to get the wow factor.

1. Give them something memorable before they leave the premises

2. Do something extraordinary after they've left

3. Follow-up multiple times - you'd be surprised how many people don't even bother to do it once

Let's look at these in more detail.

Give them something memorable before they leave

Try to imagine what it's like for someone who's looking for a care home. They've visited 3, 4, maybe even 5 homes. They get home. They're tired, and think they've done enough for today. They'll give it some more thought tomorrow.

Next evening, they decide the time has come to make a decision, or at least narrow it down to one or two that they can take Mum to see.

Trouble is, they can't remember the exact details of each home. In fact, they're all beginning to merge into one blurry mass. And the longer they leave it, the more indistinct and hazy they all become.

At this point, they'll probably look at the information each home gave them to take away, to help them remember and assist their decision-making.

Question is, what will they have from your care home?

You would not believe the number of homes that don't have anything but a business card to give to visitors when they come to look around the home. Some don't even have that!

What about you?

As part of our Full Beds Forever Complete Marketing System for Care Homes, we create a full suite of literature for our clients. This includes a small general brochure that can be widely distributed, and a full set of stationery.

We also create an A4-sized overfolder, and a set of A4-sized individual brochures representing each service the home provides (general residential, dementia, respite, nursing, etc.)

These individual brochures are high-quality items, printed on thick, glossy paper, that go into the overfolder, which itself is printed on thick card.

This gives the impression of a professional organisation that takes the matter of quality seriously. It's the opposite of the 'if they can't even repaint a tatty sign, what sort of shortcuts are they making in the standard of care Mum gets?' we mentioned earlier, in the 'first impressions' section.

When you take the time to do things right, and create the right impression, it then becomes, 'This literature looks really impressive. It must be a good company that really knows what it's doing.'

It doesn't matter whether either thought is correct or not. What matters is that's how people think, and these are the sort of shortcuts they make in their mind - so, you need to use that to your advantage.

The very least you should have is good, glossy literature, preferably that goes in an overfolder. Why? Because you also want to put other things in there as well.

Think back to the section of proof and evidence. Here are some other items you'll want to include:

- Copies of any awards you've won, or been nominated for
- Copies of certification for any professional bodies you belong to

- Photocopies of glowing testimonials and reviews you've collected, and thank you letters and cards that you've received
- A DVD or Free Report showing them what to look for and how to identify a good care home - we produce these for our clients as part of the Full Beds Forever system
- A guide to care home fee funding. You can get these for free, to give out to clients, from Care Funding Guidance

Another thing you may want to include is a competitor checklist.

Once you've done the work on your strategy, and assessed your competitors' strengths and weaknesses, you should be able to compile a list of things that a prospective client should look for when searching for a care home.

This will naturally be biased towards all the things that you provide that your competition can't. For example, if all your rooms have en-suites; you've a purpose built home that has larger rooms and corridors; a cinema; a cafe; and a large garden where outdoor activities can take place - these can all go on your list.

When the prospective new client takes the checklist to the small, 21-bed home down the road, that's been converted from an old Victorian town house, they'll do a lot of coughing and spluttering when asked about each item on the list.

The checklist should be branded with your company's information, with pre-filled ticks in all the checkboxes under your home's column. So, even if they don't use the list when they visit your competitors, it will still be there to remind them of how good your home is when they come to look at all the information they've collected during the show arounds.

Do Something Extraordinary After They've Left

If you've given them a take-away pack with all the items listed above, you'll already be streets ahead of your competition. But what else can you do to get that extra WOW factor?

Well, how about sending them a gift a day after their visit?

Imagine you've been to visit a care home. The next day, you receive a bunch of flowers from the home, saying, 'Just a little gift to say thank you for visiting us yesterday at the CHME care home. We hope to see you again soon. Best wishes, Simon Beck'.

How gobsmacked would you be? Pretty blown away, I suspect. How many other companies you've dealt with have treated you that well, just for showing an interest?

This has been used very successfully by a number of our clients, though when I first suggested it, their reactions were usually: 'I can't do that. It's going to cost me a fortune!'

Let's examine that.

If you convert one in every four visitors into a new client, and it costs you £15 for each bunch of flowers, that means you've spent £60 for each new resident. Think back to when we worked out how much you could afford to spend to attract a new client. In our example it was £1000 per new resident. This comes out of that budget.

And don't forget the value of reputation. It's highly likely that the three people who don't end up becoming a customer will still be blown away by the gift and mention it to all their family and friends, often posting it on their social media profiles. And who do you think they will remember when they're asked about a good care home?

If you implement even half the items in this book, you'll be so far ahead of your competitors that it's likely you'll have a waiting list for places in your home. So there will probably be very few people who receive the gift that don't go on to become a new customer.

The important things to bear in mind with this tactic are to give the gift purely as a thank you, and to make the gift appropriate for the person receiving it.

Follow-Up Multiple Times

Just following-up is more than some care homes do, but you're aiming to be exceptional, so even once is not good enough.

I suggest you follow-up a number of times, using different methods, like email, telephone, letter and video. As part of the bonus content that comes with the book, I've prepared a full Visit Follow-Up Checklist, which includes the full 12 ways we recommend our clients follow-up. There's also a video showing you how to create an automated, personalised follow-up video for every person that comes to look around. To download a copy of the checklist, and watch the video, visit http://www.carehomemarketingbook.com/bonuses.

Chapter 23

Where To Go From Here

I really hope you've enjoyed this book, and you're raring to go, to put things into practice in your own care home, or homes.

At the start of the book I promised I'd show you how to get your marketing done for free. That secret is in the mystery bonus chapter which you can download here:

<u>http://www.carehomemarketingbook.com/bonuses</u>

If you're the type of person that likes to learn and then do things themselves, this book is your roadmap to creating a complete marketing system for your care home.

Just methodically and consistently work through each section of the book, and start implementing.

If you need a bit of help, or would prefer someone to do it for you, here are some options we can offer you.

Option 1 - Personal Help Via My Mentoring Programme
This is a monthly online meeting where you join me live, via webcam, along with others in the group.

Each month we dive deep into one aspect of marketing your care home. As it's live, you can join in and ask me questions directly about your home and your situation.

We have 'hot seats', where we take a look at someone's marketing and go through how to improve it.

After each meeting, you'll get an additional resource that you can use in you marketing, such as a free report or template for an advert.

Visit http://mentor.carehomemarketingexpert.com

Option 2 - Go Deeper Into The Full Beds Forever Method
If you like what you've seen in the book, and want full over-the-shoulder video instructions, showing exactly how to implement each strategy and tactic, you might want to check out our Full Beds Forever Training.

This goes into much more detail than we can in the book.

Visit http://www.fullbedsforever.com

Option 3 - Complete 'Done For You' Service

Our revolutionary Full Beds Forever Outsource Marketing Department programme is unique in the care industry.

More details can be found at:
http://www.carehomemarketingexpert.com/outsource-market-ing

Option 4 - Your Choice Of Individual Services

Just want a website or Facebook advertising? Or maybe you need an advertisement creating for the local paper, or a mystery shopper exercise, to find out why people are choosing your competition?

We offer all the services mentioned in this book, and can provide you with as many, or as few, as you need.

Visit http://www.carehomemarketingexpert.com

Whatever option you choose, the most important thing is just to get started. Remember the saying: 'Dig the well before you're thirsty'. If you don't have any, or enough, marketing in place, don't wait until it's too late.

Einstein's definition of insanity is: 'to keep doing the same things and expecting a different result'. If you're already having occupancy issues, nothing will change until you do. You now know what to do, so get stuck in and make it happen.

I wish you every success and happiness.